Wilbur and Orville Wright

Alexander Graham Bell

Sir George Cayley

Robert Hutchings Goddard

Rudolph Diesel

Willy Messerschmitt and Charles A. Lindbergh

Gottlieb Daimler

MONMOUTH.
JANUARI, 2006

JOHN DAVIES

MONMOUTH.
JANUARI, 2006

The Look-It-Up Book of
TRANSPORT

BERNICE KOHN was born in Philadelphia and graduated from the University of Wisconsin. She has since been an editor and writer of children's books, with more than twenty titles to her credit.

GEORGE TUCKWELL is an English artist, who served as a fighter pilot with the Royal Air Force during World War II. He graduated from Sir John Cass College and Goldsmiths College with a National Diploma of Design. He has illustrated a number of books, and his paintings have been shown both in England and the United States.

The Look-It-Up Book of
TRANSPORT

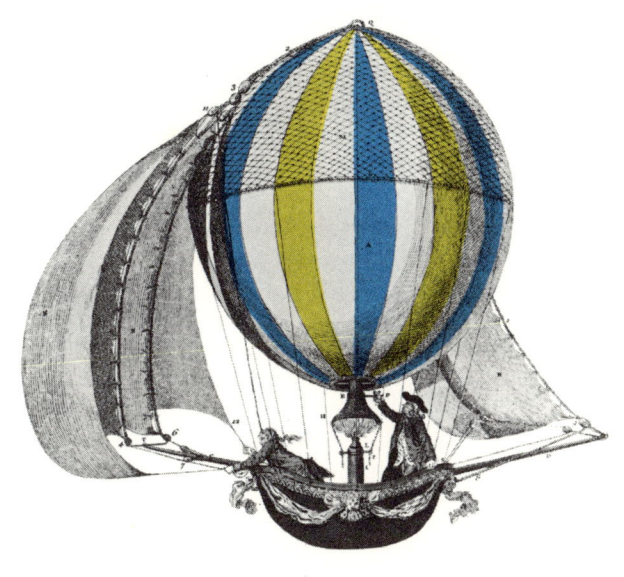

Based on an original text by Bernice Kohn
adapted by Maurice F. Allward

*Illustrated by George Tuckwell
and with photographs*

COLLINS · LONDON AND GLASGOW

American Hydrofoil, 53; British Aircraft Corporation, 17; British Airports Authority, 15; British Leyland Motor Corporation, 27, 119; British European Airways, 56; British Museum, 35 (bottom), 38 (top); British Rail, 90; British Rail, Eastern Region, 90; British Rail, Western Region, 113, 114; Cooper Union Library, 83; Cunard Line Limited, 115; Cycle World, 74; Culver Pictures, 13; Daimler-Benz, 73; Danish National Travel Office, 26; E. R. Degginger, 94; De Wys, 23, 29 (left), 30, 43, 50 (bottom), 68, 69, 77, 122; Goodyear Rubber and Tyre Company, 18; Alfred H. Gray, 92, 93; H. A. Bruno Associates, 51; Hawker Siddeley, 16, 28; Johnson Motors, 67; John La Due, 24 (lower right), 46, 66; Library of Congress, Washington, D.C., 110; London Transport Board, 125; Long Island Automotive Museum, 70; Los Angeles Airport, 75; LTV, 127; McDonnell Douglas Corporation, 17; Magnum, 36 (top), 49, 91, 103; Mansell, 21, 22 (right), 24 (lower left), 24 (upper left), 24 (upper right), 36 (bottom), 48 (top), 48 (centre), 50 (top), 82, 98; Metropolitan Museum of Art, New York, 33, 35 (top); Museum of Fine Arts, Boston, 58; NASA (National Aeronautics and Space Administration), 63, 65, 106–109; National Film Board of Canada, 59; National Film Board and Northwest Territories Tourist Office (Canada), 104; National Maritime Museum (U.S.A.), 37; NYPL, 20, 22 (centre), 22 (right), 42, 47; Novosti (U.S.S.R.), 124, 126; George A. Oliver, 71; Otis Elevator Company (U.S.A.), 44; Pan American Airways, 16 (top); Remington Art Memorial, 123 (bottom); Shaefer Brewing Company, 97; The Submarine Museum (U.S. Navy), 117, 118; Swiss National Tourist Office and Swiss Federal Railways, 29 (right), 34; Smithsonian Institution, Washington, D.C., 10, 13; Texas Eastern Transmission Corporation, 79; Trans World Airlines, 16 (centre); Union Pacific, 41, 85, 112; Union Pacific Railroad Museum Collection, 84, 86; U.S. Air Force Photo, 133; U.S. Department of Transportation and Federal Highway Administration, 81; U.S. Navy Photo, 19.

Left Endpapers: The Mansell Collection—all except: lower right, Otis Elevator Company; centre, NASA.
Right Endpapers: The Mansell Collection—all except: upper right, Culver Pictures, Inc.; centre left, courtesy of Mrs. Esther C. Goddard.

ISBN 0 00 102204 0
PRINTED AND MADE IN GREAT BRITAIN
BY C. TINLING & CO. LTD., LONDON AND PRESCOT

What is Transport?

The word *transport* comes from two Latin words that mean "to carry across". Transport carries people wherever they want to go. It brings them things they need from far away places. Transport moves people or goods across oceans, mountains, deserts or jungles. It moves on land, on water, in air, even in space and on the Moon.

The earliest form of transport was man power. Man's own two feet took him where he wanted to go. His arms or back carried his burdens. In time, he learned to pull loads on a sledge, to cross water on a simple raft, to use pack animals. He discovered how to make a canoe and the use of the wheel.

From these simple beginnings came the motor car, the ocean liner, the airliner and now the spacecraft. Once upon a time, the average person rarely travelled more than a mile or two from his birthplace. Less than 200 years ago many people were born, lived and died without ever visiting the next village. Today, following developments in transport and social changes, it is commonplace for a person to travel many thousands of miles each year.

This book describes most of the many methods of transport used to bring about the great change, which has affected the lives of everyone.

Aeroplane

An aeroplane is a mechanically-driven aircraft that is heavier than air. Apart from spacecraft the aeroplane is the fastest means of transport that we have. Many aeroplanes can travel faster than the speed of sound (about 760 miles an hour); some can go three times as fast as that. You can travel round the world in less than a day!

The first successful flight by a powered aeroplane was made on 17th December, 1903, at Kitty Hawk, North Carolina, U.S.A., when Orville Wright flew the *Flyer* for 12 seconds, covering a distance of 120 feet.

At the time, no one seemed to think it was very important and only a few newspapers reported the flight. But the Wright brothers continued to build planes and to fly. By 1905 they were able to fly twenty-four miles in thirty-eight minutes.

Everyone became excited about aeroplanes. They were built everywhere. Stunts, exhibitions and races drew huge crowds. Many pilots lost their lives in crashes but few pioneers were discouraged. Planes were improved as designers learned from their mistakes. One new model followed the other, each a little better than the one before.

However, when World War I started in 1914, military aircraft were still regarded as a novelty. The military authorities had vague ideas about using them for reconnaissance, artillery observation and patrol duties over the English Channel.

By the time the war ended four years later, aeroplanes had grown up. Pilots in fast, heavily-armed fighter aircraft had shot each other down in flames over the muddied fields of the Western Front; reconnaissance

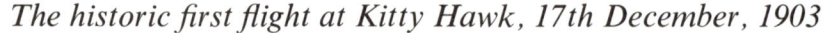

The historic first flight at Kitty Hawk, 17th December, 1903

AEROPLANES OF WORLD WAR I

NIEUPORT 28

FOKKER DR.I

NIEUPORT 17

FOKKER D.VII

ALBATROSS D.III

SPAD 13

FOKKER E.IV

VICKERS FB.9 "GUN BUS"

PFALZ D.III

SOPWITH TRIPLANE

GOTHA BOMBER

BRISTOL FIGHTER

R.E.8

SOPWITH CAMEL

DE HAVILLAND D.H.4

aeroplanes had reported the disposition of troops and munitions on the ground, and of ships at sea; bomber aeroplanes had dropped high explosive and incendiary bombs on railways, towns and villages. Dive bombers had been in action; torpedo aircraft had scored their first victories at sea.

The aeroplane was here to stay.

After the war a series of exciting long-distance flights took place, proving that aeroplanes could transport more than death and destruction. In June, 1919, the Atlantic was crossed non-stop for the first time by an aeroplane. The aeroplane was a converted Vickers Vimy bomber, flown by John Alcock and Arthur Whitten Brown. Before the end of the year another Vimy linked Britain with her farthermost dominion, Australia, for the first time. In 1924, American Air Service pilots completed the first round-the-world flight of 25,534 miles in two Douglas World Cruisers.

One of the most exciting events in the whole history of aviation took place in May, 1927. A young flyer by the name of Charles A. Lindbergh took off from New York City in *The Spirit of St. Louis*, a small Ryan monoplane. Alone he set out to fly across the Atlantic Ocean. While the whole world waited by their radios, Lindbergh succeeded brilliantly, and landed in Paris $33\frac{1}{2}$ hours after his take-off. Overnight Lindbergh became a world hero and his epic flight helped to focus attention on the possibilities and problems of aeroplanes.

Since then aeroplanes have been developed for almost every conceivable purpose; military aircraft, fighters and bombers for offence and defence; light aircraft for pleasure flying and for matters of business;

Louis Blériot makes the first flight across the English Channel on 25th July, 1909

gliders for fun; and helicopters when there is a need for aeroplanes to fly straight up and down, or hover. Most important of all, from the transport point of view, are the big commercial airliners which have made travel on a wide scale possible for millions of people.

See also: AIRSHIP; AIRLINER; AUTOGYRO; BALLOON; BLIMP; DIRIGIBLE; GLIDER; HELICOPTER; ZEPPELIN.

THE SPIRIT OF ST. LOUIS, *now in the Smithsonian Institution, Washington, D.C.*

Air Cushion Vehicle

This is the term used for a form of transport which has only been developed recently and which employs a principle fundamentally different from that of other vehicles.

Air cushion vehicles, usually called ACVs, do not run on wheels and are thus quite different from a lorry or motor car. An ACV is also distinct from a ship; it operates clear of the water and resistance to its motion is very small. Unlike aircraft, ACVs are not fitted with wings and thus do not fly in the normal manner.

As the name implies, ACVs are in fact supported on a cushion of air and travel without touching any surface. On simple vehicles the cushion of air is obtained merely by ejecting air through the underside of the body. On most practical ACVs, however, the air cushion is contained within an outer curtain of air and a plastic skirt.

This type of vehicle was pioneered in Britain. *Hovercraft*, a trade name for a particular make of ACV, are in service all over the world. Air cushion vehicles can travel over water and land, crossing from one to the other with an ease and speed not possible in other types of vehicle.

ACVs have not yet been fully developed commercially, but their use is assured in those areas impassable to wheeled vehicles.

Airliner

Airliners are aeroplanes specially designed to carry passengers, swiftly and safely, hundreds of miles.

The first aeroplane passenger, C. Furnas, was carried by Orville Wright on 14th May, 1905, in the Wright 1905 *Flyer III*. The first scheduled passenger airline began operating in 1914 between St. Petersburg and Tampa, Florida, in the United States.

In Europe, after some pioneering passenger flights, the world's first daily commercial scheduled air service opened on 25th August, 1919, between London and Paris, using converted De Havilland single-engined bombers. Passengers found the flight expensive (single fare £21), draughty, noisy and uncomfortable. Two or three wicker seats were crammed into the fuselage (where the rear gunner used to sit) for the passengers, who huddled up in leather coats, helmets and goggles.

When the Douglas DC-3 Dakota twin-engined landplane airliner appeared on the scene in 1936, the standard of comfort took a great step forward, and with it, civil air transport.

The DC-3 was followed by a series of four-engined airliners, such as the DC-4, DC-6 and DC-7, the Lockheed *Constellation* and the Boeing *Stratocruiser*. Hundreds of these fine airliners carried thousands of passengers millions of miles.

All these aircraft, which were powered by piston engines driving propellers, were soon to be rendered obsolete by a revolutionary new form

Heathrow Airport—the busiest international airport in the world

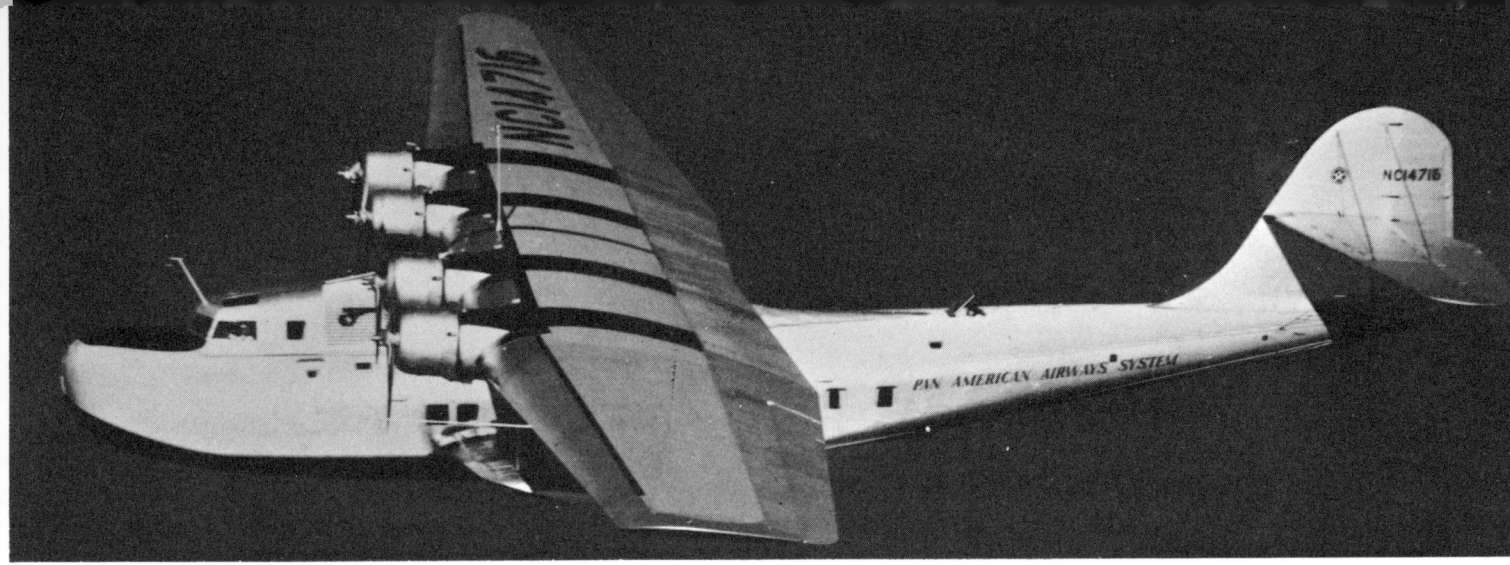

A Martin M-130 transpacific Clipper of Pan American Airways

The Lockheed Constellation—a popular airliner of the '40s and '50s

The Hawker Siddeley Trident 3B tri-jet airliner

The maiden flight of the McDonnell Douglas DC-10 airbus

The Anglo-French supersonic airliner, Concorde

of airliner—Britain's De Havilland Comet, first jet airliner in the world, with a cruising speed of 500 miles an hour, or about twice that of earlier airliners.

The importance of airliners for long-distance travel cannot be over-emphasized. In 1951 a total of 372,346 people flew the Atlantic, less than half the number that went by sea. One year later the air passengers had increased to 497,021 and in 1954 the total was 893,072—more than those carried by ship. By 1970 the last of the great ocean liners had stopped carrying passengers across the Atlantic all the year round. Nowadays most people prefer to fly. All over the world more than 300 million people travel in airliners each year.

See also: AEROPLANE; AIRSHIP; DIRIGIBLE; JET ENGINE; VTOL; ZEPPELIN.

Airship

An airship is a lighter-than-air aircraft, mechanically propelled and capable of being steered. There are three main classes of airship: rigid, where the distinctive elongated envelope is maintained by a rigid internal framework; non-rigid, where the shape is maintained by the pressure of a gas; semi-rigid, where the form is maintained by a rigid keel and the pressure of a gas.

During World War I Zeppelin airships were used by Germany to bomb London, but their effect on morale was more significant than the damage they caused. The lumbering giants, filled with highly-inflammable hydrogen gas, proved no match against swift fighter aircraft firing incendiary bullets.

After the war, in July, 1919, Britain's *R.34* was the first airship to cross the Atlantic. There were also many fine airships made in America, such as the *Shenandoah* of 1923 and the *Akron* and *Macon* in the early thirties. These American craft used helium gas which, being non-inflammable, was much safer than the hydrogen used in the Zeppelins.

In Britain airship development ceased in 1930 following the crash of the *R.101* in France, and after the Zeppelin *Hindenberg* burst into flames while being moored at Lakehurst, New Jersey, U.S.A., in May, 1937, the era of the airship came to an end.

Non-rigid airships made a brief reappearance during World War II, when they were used extensively by the United States for coastal convoy and anti-sumbarine patrol duties.

Today the few airships in existence, of the non-rigid type, are used almost exclusively for advertising. Sometimes they have the advertiser's name displayed on the side of the envelope, and sometimes they trail a banner or a streamer. In rare cases they are used for sightseeing trips.

See also: BALLOON; BLIMP; DIRIGIBLE; ZEPPELIN.

Amphibian

An amphibian is a vehicle that can be used on both land and water. A few car-boat amphibians have been made for pleasure, but most amphibians, because of their great expense, have been developed for military purposes.

Amphibious landing craft can carry soldiers over water, cruise onto the beach and continue as a land vehicle. Amphibious aircraft can operate from water and, by extending wheels, from land bases also.

Amphibious vehicles landing during World War II

Autogyro

An autogyro is a rotating-wing aircraft that has a propeller at the front of the fuselage, like a conventional aeroplane, and an overhead rotor, like a helicopter. On a helicopter, however, the rotor is powered; on an autogyro it is not. An autogyro gets its propulsion from its propeller; forward movement creates an airstream flowing through the rotor, in which the rotor spins automatically, developing lift. An autogyro cannot hover, but can take off and land nearly vertically.

Few autogyros have been built; most of those in use today are small, single-seat machines, built for pleasure.

See also: HELICOPTER; VTOL.

19

Montgolfier's first balloon, inflated with heated air, made an ascent at Annonay on 5th June, 1783

Balloon

A balloon is an airtight bag, filled with heated air or a gas lighter than air, that rises and floats in the atmosphere. It was this simple principle that enabled man to fulfil his age-old dream to fly through the air.

A French paper manufacturer, Joseph Montgolfier, invented the balloon. One day, in 1782, while sitting by his fireplace, he watched the small bits of burning matter rising up the chimney. Montgolfier thought the bits were being lifted up by a special gas coming from the fire (in fact, the pieces were being carried up by expanding warm air which was lighter than the surrounding cool air) and wondered whether, if he caught some and put it in a bag, the bag would rise? He made a small bag of silk, open at the bottom, and lit a fire of paper underneath it—and watched the bag

A sail-steered balloon, 1789

rise to the ceiling. Further tests were carried out with bigger and better bags.

For a public demonstration the following summer, Joseph and his brother Jacques Étienne, made a large balloon of linen, which they lined with paper to make it airtight. They burned charcoal under the bag until the air inside was heated. The balloon rose 6,000 feet into the air before an astonished crowd.

In the autumn of that same year, 1783, the Montgolfiers launched another balloon. This time there was a larger audience which included King Louis XVI of France. The balloon carried three living creatures; a duck, a cock and a sheep. The flight lasted eight minutes and the animals landed safely two miles away from their starting point in Versailles.

At once, excited plans were made to send a man aloft and a new balloon was ready within a month. It had a passenger platform hanging from the bottom. On it was a fire pan to heat the air inside the balloon.

On 15th October, 1783, a young scientist named Pilâtre de Rozier climbed onto the platform. The fire was started, the ground ropes were paid out, and de Rozier rose into the air. He carried a bucket of water and a sponge, and was kept busy putting out the small fires that started on the covering of the balloon. The ascent lasted for four and a half minutes and reached a height of eighty-four feet.

21

Semi-rigid hot-air balloon, 1784

François Blanchard's paddle-steered balloon

A typical hot-air balloon of 1800

On 21st November, 1783, de Rozier and a friend, the Marquis d'Arlandes, went up in a balloon that was not held by ground ropes. These men made the first free flight in history. As they dashed madly about their platform putting out the smouldering fires, their balloon reached a height of about 500 feet. The balloon drifted above the city of Paris for twenty-five minutes before settling down to earth.

Other hot-air flights were carried out with other passengers. But a French physicist, Jacques Charles, and two young mechanics, the Robert brothers, were experimenting with hydrogen-filled balloons. Hydrogen is lighter than air and thus rises without heating. On 1st December, 1783, Charles and the elder Robert brother rose in a hydrogen balloon and travelled twenty-seven miles. The age of flying had really begun.

The great disadvantage of the free balloon as a means of transport was the difficulty of controlling it. The balloonist cannot make it go in a chosen direction, except by the skilful use of air currents. In the early days many attempts were made to solve this problem by using sails, oars, rudders or paddles, but none was successful. When a controllable aircraft, the dirigible, was invented in 1852, the day of the balloon was over.

Today, relatively small balloons are widely used for weather observation duties. Large specialized balloons are also used for lifting scientific instruments above the lower atmospheric levels, to permit unobstructed observations of the sun and to measure radiation from outer space.

Surprisingly, ballooning is an increasingly popular modern sport. The balloons rise on hot air generated by gas burners, but are essentially the same as the first balloons devised by the Montgolfier brothers nearly two hundred years ago.

See also: AIRSHIP; BLIMP; DIRIGIBLE; ZEPPELIN.

Barge

A barge is a flat-bottomed roomy boat used chiefly on rivers and canals. At first barges were pulled by men, horses or oxen, walking along the bank of the river or canal. Now barges are usually towed by another vessel, or have their own engines. They are generally used to move heavy freight such as coal or rock. On large rivers, such as the River Thames, barges are used as *lighters* to load and unload ("lighten") ships.

The name barge is also given to the special motor boats used by captains and flag officers in the Royal Navy, and to a type of small sailing boat called the Thames sprit-sail barge.

Bicycle

The two most widespread and important means of land transport are undoubtedly the railway and the motor car. Of the lesser forms of transport, however, the bicycle is the firm favourite.

The first recognizable ancestor of the modern bicycle made its appearance in Paris around 1790. It was called a *célérifère*, or "horse on wheels", and consisted of a wooden body mounted on two wheels, with one end carved in the shape of an animal's head. It was operated by the feet and could not be steered.

In spite of its limitations, the *célérifère* proved remarkably popular, spreading throughout France to England and, by 1819, to New York.

English hobbyhorse, 1819

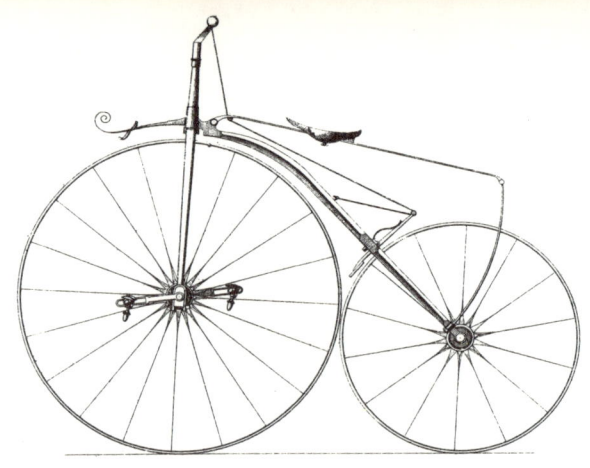
Velocipede

Rover safety bicycle, 1885

The popular bicycle of today

By this time it had springs under the seat for comfort and a handlebar that steered the front wheel. With these improvements it was called the *draisine* in Europe and the *dandyhorse* in America. In Britain it was often known as the *hobbyhorse*. A fast rider could go at 8 miles an hour!

In 1839, a Scot, Kirkpatrick Macmillan, improved the *draisine* further by fitting a complex set of levers to drive the wheel. He should have gone on to discover the pedal, but failed to do so.

The invention of the pedal was left to a Frenchman, Pierre Michaux. His revolutionary development appeared in 1861. The new machine was called the *velocipede*. The huge front wheel had pedals on it, and there was a very small wheel behind. The velocipede was difficult and dangerous to ride but extremely popular nevertheless.

In 1880, an Englishman, Harry Lawson, thought of putting the pedals between the wheels with a chain to drive the rear one. So the bicyle was really born.

Later improvements—light frames, rubber tyres, ball bearings, good brakes—made the bicycle so popular that by 1900 there were ten million in France alone.

From then until now, bicycles have been in use throughout most of the world both for sport and as a major means of transport.

Bicycle designs remained virtually unchanged for over half a century until the early 1960s, when Britain introduced the idea of using much smaller wheels for easier cycling under average conditions.

See also: MOTOR CYCLE; MOTOR SCOOTER.

Blimp

A blimp was a small non-rigid airship, or dirigible, used widely in World War I. The gas bag had no frame and was loose and floppy when not fully filled with gas. For this reason, these craft were often referred to as *limps* in Britain. For a time, the best known model was a B-limp, which was very soon altered to blimp.

See also: AIRSHIP; BALLOON; DIRIGIBLE; ZEPPELIN.

Boat

Boat is the term usually applied to any relatively small open craft which is used on water and moved by oars, paddles, or a motor, and which is not engaged in ocean service. A fifty-foot cruiser is called a boat, even though it may carry its own *smaller* boat.

Canoes, rowing boats, sailing boats, yachts, houseboats, sampans, kayaks are all boats. So are the bundles of reeds tied together, formerly used in Egypt, the big bowls made of wicker covered with pitch and horsehide that are used in Central America, and the vessels made of woven reeds that are used in South America.

See also: CANOE; GALLEY; GONDOLA; HYDROFOIL; JUNK; KAYAK; MOTOR BOAT; RAFT; ROWING BOAT; SAILING SHIPS AND BOATS; SAMPAN; UMIAK; YACHT.

Boat Train

A boat train is a normal train that makes part of its journey on a ferry boat. Passengers usually leave the train while travelling on the boat, unless the crossing is at night and they are asleep. Freight naturally remains loaded during the crossing. The advantage of a boat train is the increased convenience; passengers and freight do not have to be unloaded

The boat train running between Denmark and Germany

from the train and then loaded onto the ship; with the reverse procedure on arrival.

A boat train may also be a special train, carrying passengers from the big city centres to their connections on the coast with cross-channel ferries or transatlantic liners.

See also: FERRY BOAT.

Bus

A bus is a public road vehicle designed to carry a relatively large number of passengers. The word is shortened from the early term "omnibus", which itself is derived from the Latin *omnis* meaning all.

Early buses were all single-deckers, but to accommodate more passengers extra seats were installed on the roof. At first the upper deck passengers sat in the open, exposed to the elements, but now almost all double-deckers have the upper deck enclosed. The exceptions are some buses at holiday resorts which have open, upper decks. These give holiday-makers an uninterrupted view, and at the same time give them the thrill of travelling "like it was in the old days".

An early London bus

The modern Leyland "Leopard" long-distance bus

In the early 1930s, the rear-engined bus appeared and, a little later, for reasons of economy, buses switched from petrol fuel to diesel oil.

Today a wide variety of buses are produced to suit differing conditions all over the world. Most famous, perhaps, are the red double-deckers used by London Transport.

See also: STEAM CARRIAGE; TROLLEY BUS.

Business Jet

Business jets are the small jet aircraft used by large corporations and business executives.

Although the scheduled airlines operate excellent and regular services

27

to most major cities and industrial centres, the times of the services are often inconvenient and the airports served are sometimes a considerable distance from the final destination of many businessmen.

A company-owned aircraft overcomes both these problems; it can leave whenever its passengers desire, and can operate into the many hundreds of smaller airfields not served by regular airlines. Many business aircraft are still propeller-driven, but growing congestion in the skyways has made the ownership of a jet-powered aircraft an advantage. Jets fly their occupants at the speed of a scheduled airliner and thus they fit into the normal traffic patterns.

See also: AEROPLANE; AIRLINER; EXECUTIVE JET; JET ENGINE.

The Hawker Siddeley HS 125 business jet

Cable Car

A cable car is a form of bus that has no power of its own. As its name implies, the vehicle is attached to a cable which pulls it along. Andrew S. Hallidie invented the cable car in 1873.

The cable cars of San Francisco are world famous. The hills of the city are so steep that ordinary trolley buses cannot climb them. The San Francisco cable cars run on tracks, and the cable that pulls them runs in a slot below the level of the street.

Cable cars of a completely different kind are widely used in mountain-

Cable car, San Francisco, U.S.A.   *Cable car, Valais, Switzerland*

ous regions, the cars being supported by and running along strong cables stretched between steel towers leading from the floors of valleys to mountain peaks. Such cable cars usually operate in pairs, so that the weight of the ascending car is counterbalanced by the descending car.

See also: CHAIR LIFT; FUNICULAR; SKI LIFT.

Canoe

A canoe is a long, narrow boat, pointed at both ends, which is propelled by one or more paddles. The paddler (or paddlers) always faces the bow and uses the paddle for both propulsion and steering. Canoes are fast, easy to handle and relatively light.

Most canoes are made by stretching a covering over a light framework of wood or other material. The Eskimo canoe is usually made of sealskin on a frame of wood, whalebone or other bone. American Indians made their canoes of birchbark. They peeled the bark from the trees in long strips and sewed the strips together. The connected strips were then

sewn to a wooden frame and the seams sealed with hot pitch. The American Indians of the south-west had no birch trees and so they made *dugout* canoes instead. They chose a large tree trunk about three feet thick and burned out the inside until only a shell was left. Then they scraped the charred wood smooth with seashells or sharp stones. This method was also widely used in other countries.

Canoes are popular all over the world today even though they are not now a major means of transport except in primitive areas. They are used mainly for pleasure trips on lakes and rivers by hunters, fishermen, campers and other sportsmen. Modern canoes are rarely hand-made. They are manufactured from many different materials including wood, canvas, light metals, fibreglass and plastic.

See also: KAYAK; UMIAK.

Caravan

Originally the term *caravan* referred to a group of people travelling together for security on a journey through a desert or hostile region. Today, the word refers to a mobile home towed behind a motor car. Usually a caravan is quite small, consisting of one or two tiny compartments, cleverly fitted with furniture and kitchen equipment, and used for pleasure purposes. However, some people live in caravans permanently. Some of these are very large and contain a living-room, bedrooms, a kitchen and a bathroom. These may be considered more as wheeled homes than caravans.

A special form of caravan is the popular motor caravan. This is basically a small goods vehicle with the rear section fitted out as a caravan in which people can eat and sleep in remarkable comfort while on holiday.

Typical 4-berth caravan

Volkswagen motor-caravan

Carriage

A carriage is an open horse-drawn vehicle. From the 1700s until the invention of the motor car the carriage was widely used in most countries as a means of transport. Unlike the coach, it was designed for speed,

CHAISE

LANDAU

VICTORIA

BROUGHAM

CALASH

CABRIOLET

HANSOM CAB

Whisket du Chasse, 1788

elegance and grace. Carriages were often made of fine woods, handsomely decorated, with the hardware and fittings made of finely wrought metal. At first the wheels had iron tyres, but after 1875 these were replaced with solid rubber tyres.

Carriage development was very rapid in England, where expert craftsmen produced lighter and lighter vehicles. A wide range of these vehicles was produced and many were exported abroad.

There were many different types of carriage, ranging from small two-wheelers such as the Chaise and Cabriolet, to the four-wheel Brougham and the popular Hansom Cab.

The four-wheel Brougham, built initially for Lord Brougham in 1839, was a sturdy two-seater which became the favourite carriage of doctors and other professional men who were too staid to use lighter, more flamboyant types. The Hansom Cab, called after its inventor, Joseph Hansom, was a light, open two-seater used for hire purposes. Seated on a highly-elevated box behind, the driver communicated with the passengers through a hole in the roof.

See also: CHARIOT; COACH; COVERED WAGON; STAGECOACH; WAGON.

Catamaran

Originally the term was used to describe a raft made of three or more logs lashed together for use in surf by the natives of Madras, India.

Nowadays a catamaran is a vessel with two hulls joined together by a rigid frame.

Modern catamaran sailing vessels are popular as they are very fast; the world speed record of over 30 miles an hour is held by a catamaran. The wide beam gives excellent stability, and the twin hulls provide plenty of space for accommodation and provisions.

See also: TRIMARAN; YACHT.

Chair Lift

A chair lift, high in the mountains of Switzerland

A chair lift is a series of chairs, suspended from a continuous cable running over pulley assemblies mounted on steel towers, leading to the tops of hills or the upper slopes of a mountain. They are widely used in winter holiday resorts catering for ski-ing enthusiasts. The chairs, holding one or two persons, transport skiers to the tops of the various ski slopes, ready for the downward run.

See also: CABLE CAR; FUNICULAR; SKI LIFT.

An Etruscan chariot

Chariot

The chariot was the first practical wheeled vehicle. The ancient Sumerians of Mesopotamia are thought to have invented the wheel about 6,000 years ago. Early wheels were probably merely a slice from a log, or three planks of wood pegged together to form a disc. These wore away quickly and soon a strengthening metal band was added to the rim. Then the wheel was lightened, first by cutting away unwanted wood, and finally by fitting spokes.

The chariot used by the Sumerians was a small, clumsy, two-wheeled cart. Drawn by wild asses, initially they were used only by priests and nobles. The use of carts to transport goods came much later. This type of cart was used for a thousand years, with little change.

Then, with the introduction of the horse from Central Asia, a relatively light, fast, horse-drawn chariot made its appearance. Introduced into Egypt by early invaders, the Hyksos, it consisted of a small platform with a railing or enclosure at the sides and the front. The back was open and the rider stood to drive.

An Assyrian chariot

The new chariot became a major weapon of the warlike Assyrians, and was also used by the Greeks and the Romans. In battle, the driver tied the horses' reins round his waist so that his hands were free to

A Greek chariot

handle weapons. War chariots were also used extensively in ancient Britain.

See also: CARRIAGE; COACH; WAGON.

Roman racing chariots

Clipper Ship

Clipper ships were so named because they "clipped along" at a great speed, and represented the peak of glory of the sailing ship. They had long narrow hulls, knife-sharp bows and a vast area of canvas, for the greatest possible speed.

Clipper ships were developed to meet the demand for fresh tea from the Indies, and they came into their own when the discovery of gold in North America and Australia started a huge rush of immigrants to both countries. They were also used to transport wool from the great sheep farms of Australia.

The first fully-rigged ship with clipper lines was the *Glentanar* built by Hall of Aberdeen in 1842. This was developed from the schooner *Scottish Maid* also built by Hall in 1839.

The first American clipper ship was the *Rainbow* of 1845. It, and the other clipper ships which followed, such as Britain's famous *Cutty Sark*, were magnificent craft which captured the imagination of all those who loved the sea.

Their speed and manoeuvrability are legend. Outsailing any naval vessel, they could cross the Atlantic in 14 days and, rounding Cape Horn, sail from New York to San Francisco in as little as 89 days—a record set by the *Flying Cloud*. The previous sailing time had been 180 days.

The beautiful and efficient clipper ships ruled the seas for only ten years. They were rendered obsolete by the steady development of ocean-going steamships, and by the opening of the Suez Canal in 1869.

See also: SAILING SHIPS AND BOATS; SCHOONER; SHIP; WINDJAMMER.

Coach

A coach is a large, closed, four-wheeled vehicle, having doors in the side and a raised seat at the front for the driver. The name comes from the town of Kocs, in Hungary, where coaches were built in the middle of the fifteenth century.

The story of the coach in Britain reaches its peak in the years after 1800, when a magnificent system of mail coaches was running on all the main roads. The specialized mail coach used was invented in 1742 by John Palmer of Bath. As a boy Palmer had noticed that the post-boys,

A medieval coach

arriving with the mails from London, took no less than 38 hours to cover the 109 miles, while the horse-drawn post-chaises took only half that time. Palmer proposed that special fast coaches should run along all the main roads, each carrying a guard armed with two loaded blunderbusses. The driver was also to carry two pistols. The first mail coach was merely

An 18th century English mail coach

a light post-chaise pressed into service, but later coaches were designed specially for the service. To give them greater speed than the stage coaches, it was arranged to change the horses every eight miles instead of the normal sixteen.

The most elaborate coaches were those used by royalty and the nobility. The interiors of these were richly decorated with velvets and satins, while the trimmings were often of pure gold. The elaborate art of this type of coach reached its zenith in the coaches specially designed for the coronations of the kings of Great Britain and France. Survivors of these priceless coaches are today used only for ceremonial processions.

See also: CARRIAGE; CHARIOT; COVERED WAGON; STAGECOACH; WAGON.

Coracle

A primitive form of small boat. Usually round in shape, it consists of a skeleton of wood covered with the hides of animals, such as horses and buffaloes. Various kinds of coracles are still in use among primitive people throughout the world.

See also: CANOE; KAYAK; UMIAK.

Covered Wagon

The rugged wagons used by American pioneers when they migrated to the West were usually protected by a distinctive canvas covering stretched over curved wooden ribs. This led to the term "covered wagon" being applied to any type of wagon with a canvas cover.

See also: CARRIAGE; CHARIOT; COACH; STAGECOACH; WAGON.

Crawler

Crawler is the name given to the giant tracked vehicles used to transport America's Saturn V rockets, complete with Apollo spacecraft on top, from the building in which they are assembled and checked to the launching pad.

The crawlers are the biggest land vehicles in the world, being 131 feet long by 114 feet wide and weighing over 3,000 tons. The track units are 10 feet high and 40 feet long; each track link is nearly 8 feet long and weighs one ton.

Their speed is less than one mile per hour so that the $3\frac{1}{2}$-mile trip to the launching pad takes about 7 hours. (*See illustration at left on page 107.*)

See also: TRACKED VEHICLES.

Diesel-Electric Locomotive

A diesel-electric locomotive is a locomotive which uses a diesel-oil internal combustion engine coupled to a generator which supplies power to the electric traction motors which in turn drive the wheels.

Such locomotives are some four or five times as efficient as the steam locomotives they replaced, as well as being more flexible, smaller and cleaner. Another advantage is that the number of multiple-unit driving axles that can be concentrated under the control of one operator permits rapid acceleration. These characteristics make electric drive far superior to steam in hilly regions or where frequent stops are required.

The first diesel-electric trains were used in the United States as early as 1934 to draw crack passenger trains. Today, nearly all locomotives are of this type.

See also: INTERNAL COMBUSTION ENGINE; RAILWAY; STEAM LOCOMOTIVE.

A 3-unit diesel-electric locomotive hauling freight in the United States

Diesel-Hydraulic Locomotive

Like the diesel-electric locomotive, the diesel-hydraulic is powered by a diesel-oil internal combustion engine. The difference is that whereas on the diesel-electric locomotive the wheels are operated by electricity generated by the engine, on the diesel-hydraulic locomotive the wheels are turned directly by the engine. An ordinary clutch and gear box would never stand up to railway work, and the diesel-hydraulic locomotive has a specially developed hydraulic clutch.

Diesel-hydraulic locomotives are mainly used for shunting and short-run duties.

See also: ELECTRIC LOCOMOTIVE; INTERNAL COMBUSTION ENGINE; RAILWAY; STEAM LOCOMOTIVE.

Dirigible

A dirigible is an airship that has a gas-filled bag and can be steered or navigated. (The word *dirigible* comes from a Latin word meaning "steerable".)

Gaston Tissandier's first electric-powered dirigible

In 1852, Pierre Julienn, a French clockmaker, built the first dirigible which had rudders and stern elevators. This dirigible was never actually flown but, in the same year, Henri Giffard, who had borrowed many of Julienn's ideas did make the first motor-driven flight from Paris to Trappes, seventeen miles away. The balloon was shaped like a rugby ball, 143 feet long, and powered by a 3 horse-power steam engine and a propeller.

In 1883, Gaston Tissandier built and flew an electrically-powered dirigible, but it was underpowered and not successful. The following year Captains Charles Renard and Arthur Krebs collaborated to build and fly the first really practical dirigible, the electrically-powered *La France*.

The first dirigible to use an internal combustion engine was built by the Brazilian pioneer, Alberto Santos-Dumont. He made several spectacular flights over Paris in 1898 in small craft powered by tiny petrol-driven tricycle engines. Two years later the first of the giant Zeppelins took to the air.

See also: AIRSHIP; BALLOON; BLIMP; ZEPPELIN.

Electric Locomotive

An electric locomotive is one that runs on electricity supplied from an external source, although a few early examples were powered by internal batteries. The current reaches the locomotive either from an overhead cable or from an electrified third rail.

The first electric locomotive was built by a German engineer Werner von Siemens. It was exhibited at a trade fair in 1879 and reached the speed of 5 miles an hour.

It was not until 1893 that electric locomotives went into service when, on the slopes of the Jungfrau mountain, the Swiss put into operation a railway that in less than an hour climbed from 7,000 feet to 10,000 feet. The current was supplied by an overhead line. In 1895 the first electric locomotive went into service in the United States, and from that time on they began to take the place of the steam locomotive, which despite compound engines, superheated steam and mechanical stoking with coal or oil, was inefficient and cumbersome. It was also both costly and time-consuming to run.

Electric traction overcame these problems, particularly where electric power was cheap and abundant. A modern electric locomotive is about 26 feet long and weighs about 70 tons. A steam locomotive of the same power would weigh about twice as much.

A major advantage of electric locomotives is that the power is easily and simply controlled at all speeds. They are also very reliable and give a rapid acceleration, which is ideal where frequent stops have to be made.

See also: DIESEL-ELECTRIC LOCOMOTIVE; DIESEL-HYDRAULIC LOCOMOTIVE; INTERNAL COMBUSTION ENGINE; RAILWAYS; STEAM LOCOMOTIVE.

Escalator

A modern escalator

The first escalator, exhibited in Paris, 1900

An escalator is a moving stairway. Passengers stand on a step which carries them up or down. Operated by electric motors, the steps are attached to a belt which goes round and round. At the top and bottom the moving step merges with the level of the surrounding floor.

The first escalator was built by the American Otis Elevator Company for the Paris Exposition of 1900. The following year the same escalator was removed and installed in Gimbel Brothers' department store in Philadelphia, Pennsylvania. It remained in service until 1939, when it was replaced by a more modern one.

Escalators are used not only to save people the labour of climbing up or going down stairs, but also where large numbers of people have to be moved rapidly. Escalators are often installed in big stores for the convenience of customers, and are also widely used in underground railway systems where it is necessary to move thousands of people quickly from street level to the trains.

An average escalator can carry 5,000 persons an hour.

See also: MOVING PAVEMENT.

Executive Jet

A small jet aeroplane used by business people to travel quickly and conveniently to important meetings.

See also: BUSINESS JET.

Ferry Boat

A ferry is a boat used to carry passengers or goods regularly across a river, lake or other small body of water. Before the days of bridges, ferries were used extensively, the simplest ferry being a log raft propelled by a man with a pole.

Some of the largest ferry boats are used on the busy services operating across stretches of water such as the English Channel, Lake Constance and the Scandinavian fjords. Many can carry cars as well as passengers.

As ferry boats usually only ply back and forth, they are often designed so that they can travel equally well in both directions. Doors at both ends permit loading and unloading from either end, avoiding the delay involved in turning round.

Norwegian car-and-passenger ferry

Ferry boats may run on any kind of power. Large ones usually have diesel or steam engines. Small ferry boats are often operated by ropes pulled by men or animals.

See also: BOAT TRAIN.

Funicular

A form of cable-operated railway, in which the ascending and descending cars counterbalance each other in weight. Funiculars are extensively used in mountainous regions.

See also: CABLE CAR; CHAIR LIFT; SKI LIFT.

Galleon

A galleon was a large sailing ship developed in the 15th century. They had sturdy hulls, with high "castles" at the bow and stern, and distinctive square sails set on three or four masts. Later galleons had sprit-sails and topsails for more speed. Most galleons had cannon on three or four gun decks to provide defence against privateers. In those days there was little distinction between merchantmen and warships.

Many galleons were wrecked round the coast of Britain, after the defeat

Galleons and galleasses of the Spanish Armada

of the Spanish Armada by Sir Francis Drake, as they tried to return to Spain by rounding the north of Scotland.

See also: SAILING SHIPS AND BOATS; SHIP; WARSHIP.

Galley

A galley was a large, low, open ship, propelled by both oars and sails. It was in use throughout the Middle Ages, especially in the Mediterranean.

Galleys were extensively used by merchants to transport cargoes. They were also developed into effective warships. In ancient times a warship was useless if it depended upon sail for speed. The result was the war galley, which depended mainly on oars for its motive power. The chief weapon of these ships was a deadly spike projecting from the bow, which was used to ram opposing ships.

The oars were up to fifty feet long and there were usually at least fifty of them. Sometimes as many as six men pulled each oar. The oarsmen were often slaves or captured prisoners of war, who were chained in their places.

See also: BOAT; ROWING BOAT; SHIP; WARSHIP.

Monoreme—a galley with one bank of oars

Bireme—a galley with two banks of oars

Trireme—a galley with three banks of oars

Glider

A single-seat glider

A glider is an aircraft that has no engine. Although gliders, towed behind powered aircraft, were used to transport troops and supplies during World War II, today gliding is essentially a sport.

The first successful aeroplane in history was a glider. This was a model made in 1804 by the English pioneer Sir George Cayley. In 1809 Cayley built a full-size glider, which carried a boy a few yards. Longer flights with triplane gliders were achieved with his reluctant coachman as "test pilot" in 1853.

In 1891 Otto Lilienthal of Germany began to fly his gliders. He became very skilful and had made about 2,500 glides before he stalled and crashed to his death in 1896. Other glider pioneers included the Wright brothers, who went on to fit an engine to one of their gliders and thus achieved powered flight.

Being unpowered, a glider needs assistance to launch it into the air. Winching is probably the most widely used method, but towing by aeroplanes has the advantage of being able to pull the glider to a greater height.

Once launched a glider descends relative to the air. If a glider appears to climb, it is because the mass of surrounding air is rising faster than the

Otto Lilienthal preparing for a flight

glider is sinking. Efficient gliders with a relatively flat glide and able to gain height in even weak thermals are called sailplanes.

See also: AEROPLANE.

Gondola

Gondola is the name of the elegant, long, narrow boat with a high prow and stern, used as a water-taxi in Venice, the Italian city which has canals instead of streets.

The gondolier stands up in his boat and propels it by using a long pole.

Helicopter

A helicopter can be described as an aircraft with rotating wings. On ordinary aircraft the lift is obtained by pushing the complete machine along bodily. On a helicopter, however, the necessary movement through the air is obtained by rotating the wings—which is what the blades of the overhead rotor really are. A helicopter can thus rise and descend vertically, and hover in the air without forward movement.

The lift obtained from the rotor of a helicopter not only produces a force acting vertically upwards to support the weight of the machine; it also provides the horizontal thrust required for forward flight. This explains the nose-down attitude of helicopters in normal forward flight.

A large twin-rotor passenger-carrying helicopter—the Boeing V107-11

Helicopters have proved extremely useful in war, where they have sometimes replaced army trucks for front-line transport duties. Helicopters carry troops and supplies to the battle area, and evacuate casualties.

The helicopter has also proved itself in other emergencies, such as transporting relief supplies to areas devastated by earthquakes or floods. Helicopters are also used for crop spraying, and for the erection and maintenance of electricity power supply lines.

See also: AUTOGYRO; VTOL.

Horse

After man learned to tame it, the horse became an important means of transport. At first horses were used to help men to hunt and to wage war more effectively. Then they were used to carry goods in packs slung over their backs. So popular did the pack horse become that the period from about 1200 to 1500 is sometimes known as the 'age of the pack horse'.

With the invention of the wheel horses were also used to pull chariots and light wagons, but the early forms of harness, which tended to strangle a beast if it pulled too hard, prevented heavy loads being drawn. The invention of the rigid horse collar, enabled a horse to pull a much heavier load. The collar rested on the beast's shoulders so that it could pull without harming itself.

After the Middle Ages the iron horseshoe, which had been known since Roman times, came into regular use, improving the performance of the horse under working conditions. The combined use of the harness, iron horseshoes, wheeled vehicles and, eventually, a good system of metalled roads created, particularly in England, a means of transport which reigned supreme until the invention of the railway.

Hovercraft

A particular make of air cushion vehicle.

See also: AIR CUSHION VEHICLE.

Hydrofoil

A hydrofoil is a boat which skims along above the surface of the water. The boat is mounted on wing-shaped slats, called *hydrofoils*, which extend below the bottom of the hull. The hydrofoils are shaped and set at an angle like an aeroplane wing, so that as the boat moves forward, pressures are created which lift the hull out of the water. The hydrofoil surfaces always stay under water, as does the propeller.

Hydrofoils are fast; speeds of 70 miles an hour are common, and because they are unaffected by choppy water, hydrofoils give a smooth ride. It achieves its high speed because the hull of the boat does not have to be pushed through the water. At low speeds the boat rides on the water in the normal way, but as soon as the speed is great enough to cause

The hull of the hydrofoil is lifted clear of the water, thus reducing resistance

a lifting action on the hydrofoils, the hull rises several feet above the surface.

The first hydrofoil was built by an Italian, Enrico Forlanini, in 1906. Twelve years later Dr. Alexander Graham Bell built a hydrofoil which reached a speed of 70 miles an hour, a record which remained unbroken until the 1960s.

The Soviet Union was the first country to use hydrofoil craft on a large scale and today large numbers of craft carrying up to 100 passengers are in regular use on great rivers such as the Volga. In the United States hydrofoils are used by the Navy and the Coast Guard. In Britain a hydrofoil service is operated between the mainland and the Isle of Wight during the busy summer months.

Ice Skates

Although we think of ice skating chiefly as a sport, it was an ancient means of transport. Archaeologists have discovered ice skates made of animal bone and, in Siberia, some made of walrus tusks.

Early skates were strapped to shoes, but modern skates have their own boots attached.

Ice Yacht

An ice yacht is a framework, usually triangular, supported on skates and propelled by sails. Ice yachts are used only for pleasure and are very fast—a speed of 140 miles an hour has been recorded. The sport of ice yachting originated in the Netherlands and along the Baltic coast.

See also: LAND YACHT.

Internal Combustion Engine

The internal combustion engine is not, of course, a means of transport, but because it is used in so many kinds of vehicles it deserves a special mention. Internal combustion engines power millions of cars, lorries, boats and aeroplanes.

Internal means *inside* and combustion means *burning* and the phrase "internal combustion" was used to describe engines where combustion actually took place inside the piston cylinders; in steam engines the fire is, of course, outside the pistons.

The first practical internal combustion engine was the small, gas piston engine invented by the Frenchman, Jean Joseph Étienne Lenoir. But it was the German, Nikolaus August Otto who brought out his four-stroke cycle "silent engine" in 1876 and made the internal combustion engine a success. This early model has led directly to the engines we use today.

The four-stroke cycle, sometimes referred to as "suck, squeeze, bang, blow", is the secret of the efficiency and simplicity of the modern engine. A typical internal combustion engine contains four or more pistons sliding smoothly in cylinders. When a piston moves down it *sucks* in a mixture of air and fuel. On the upstroke it compresses or *squeezes* the mixture. When it reaches the top of its stroke an electric spark ignites the explosive mixture; the result is a *bang* which forces the piston down. On the upstroke the piston expels or *blows* out the residue of the explosion from the exhaust, and is ready for the next cycle.

HOW AN INTERNAL COMBUSTION ENGINE WORKS

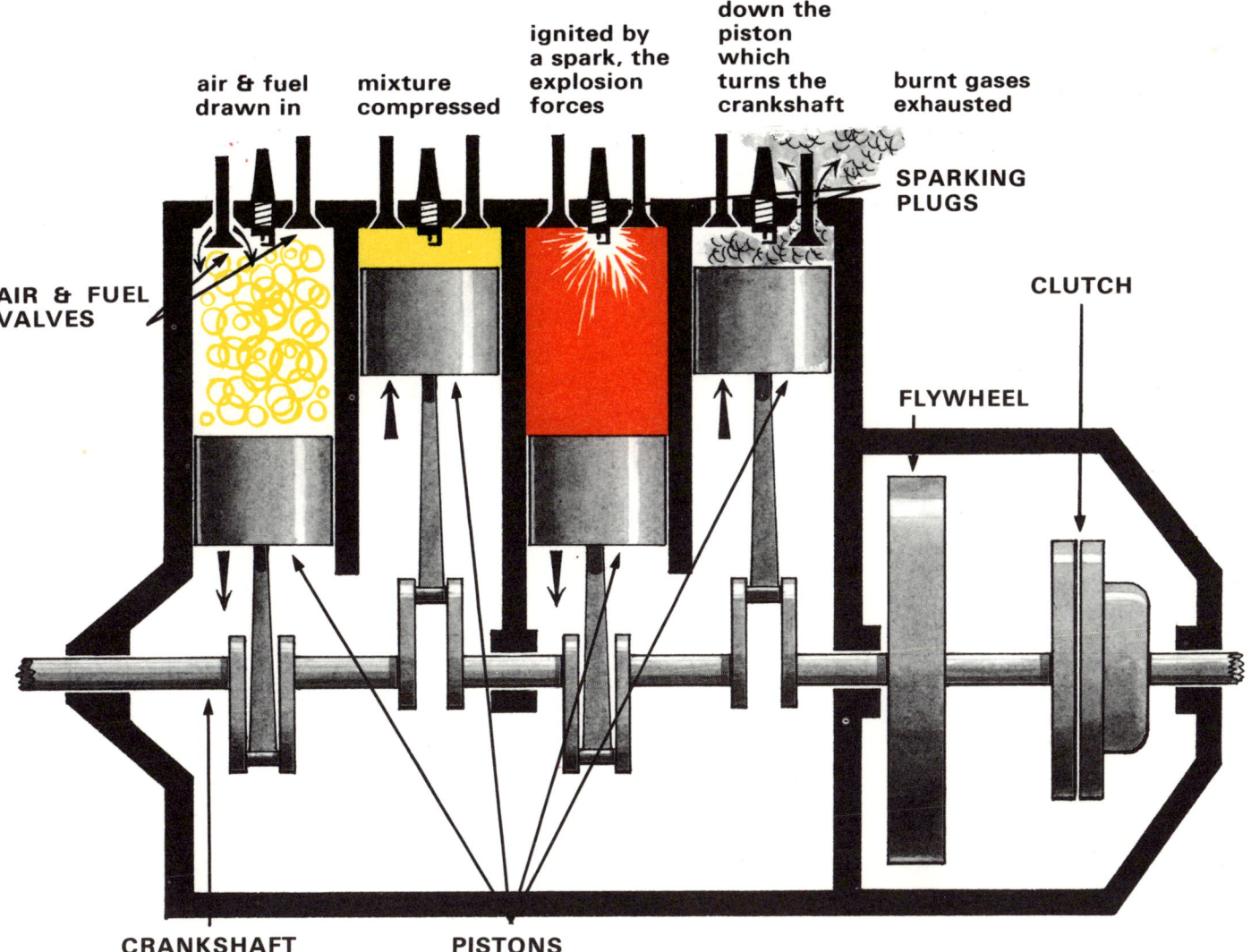

air & fuel drawn in

mixture compressed

ignited by a spark, the explosion forces

down the piston which turns the crankshaft

burnt gases exhausted

SPARKING PLUGS

AIR & FUEL VALVES

CLUTCH

FLYWHEEL

CRANKSHAFT

PISTONS

Each piston is attached to a rod, the other end of which is attached to a crankshaft. As the pistons go up and down, the crankshaft goes round and round. Gears and shafting connect the rotating crank to the wheels of a vehicle, or the propeller shaft of a boat or aeroplane.

The speed of an internal combustion engine is varied by controlling the amount of air and fuel admitted to the cylinders; the more fuel, the bigger the explosion, the faster the speed.

Since an internal combustion engine gets very hot from the burning fuel, it has to be cooled, either by water or air.

Most of the engines used in motor cars and aeroplanes run on petrol fuel, but those in lorries and boats run on diesel oil, which, although a less efficient fuel, is much cheaper. The diesel engine was invented by Rudolph Diesel, who was born in Paris in 1858. Diesel was interested in a heavy oil produced from coal, and in 1893 expressed his ideas for an engine using such an oil.

See also: AIRLINER; MOTOR BOAT; MOTOR CAR.

Jet Engine

The jet engine is not a means of transport by itself but, like the internal combustion engine, it plays an important part in moving people and goods.

The jet engine works by sucking air in at one end, compressing it, mixing it with fuel and then burning it. The hot air expands, rushes out of the tail pipe and as it does so the engine is thrust forward. The air rushing out of the tail pipe flows past a turbine wheel, spinning it rapidly. The wheel is attached to a shaft, at the front end of which is a compressor. As the turbine spins, so does the compressor, which squeezes more air being drawn in at the front, to repeat the cycle.

The jet engine is thus basically much simpler than the piston engine, in which the pistons jerk up and down at great speed, setting up severe strains and vibration. The compressor and turbine of a jet engine spin smoothly, like a top.

There are three main types of jet engine. The most common is the *turbojet*. This is the basic engine, which sucks air in at one end, and shoots it out of the other end. Sometimes a turbojet has two turbine wheels, each of which spins a separate compressor.

Trident tri-jet airliners at Heathrow Airport, London

TURBOJET ENGINE

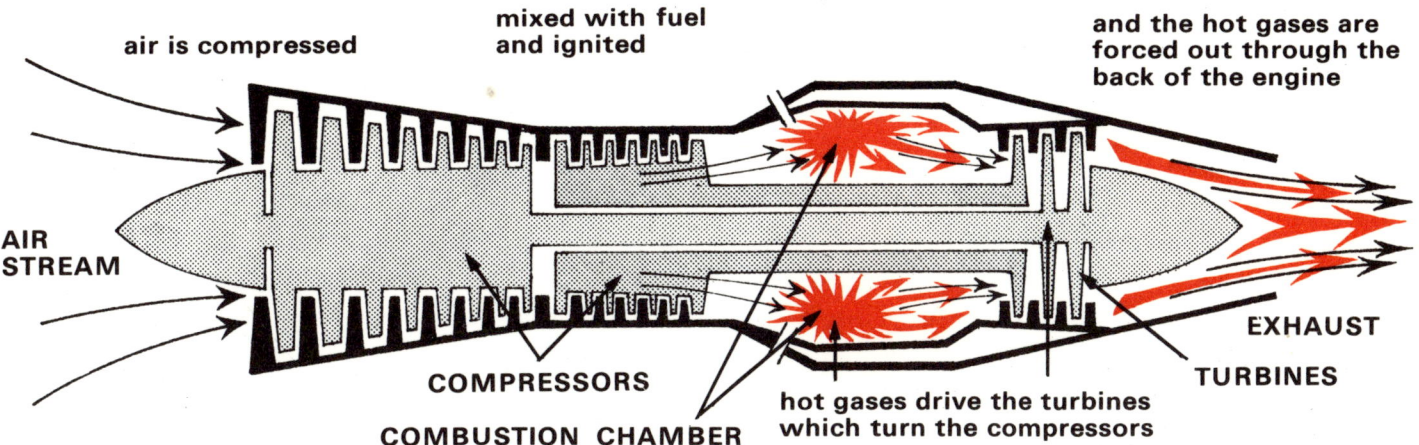

air is compressed

mixed with fuel and ignited

and the hot gases are forced out through the back of the engine

AIR STREAM

COMPRESSORS

COMBUSTION CHAMBER

hot gases drive the turbines which turn the compressors

EXHAUST

TURBINES

A *turboprop* is a jet engine that drives a propeller. This type of jet engine also usually has two turbines. One drives the compressor, and the other drives the propeller by means of gearing. With a turboprop, most of the work of driving the aircraft through the air is done by the propeller, although it also gets help from the jet exhaust.

The latest and most important type of jet engine is the *turbofan*. This has two or more turbines. One or more drives the compressors, and the other one is used to turn a big fan at the front of the engine. This type of engine gets part of its thrust from the hot gases rushing out of the exhaust but most of it comes from the mass of air pushed back by the big fan at the front, as the propeller does in the case of the turboprop. In fact, the fan on a turbofan engine may be regarded as a multi-bladed propeller.

In 1930 Frank Whittle took out the first patent on the basic features of a modern-type turbojet. On 27th August, 1939, the first jet aeroplane, a Heinkel He 178, flew with a turbojet engine providing the means of propulsion. Britain's first jet plane flight followed in 1941. The first American jet plane was the experimental Bell XP-59A, which made its trial flight in 1942.

All the early jet planes were military aircraft, but after the war jet engines were put to peaceful purposes. First came the turboprop airliners, such as the Viscount, Britannia, Electra and Vanguard. These were followed by the De Havilland Comet, the first turbojet airliner in the world.

The Comet went into service in 1952 and set revolutionary standards of speed and comfort. It quickly made all other airliners, particularly those powered by noisy, vibrating piston engines, obsolescent. In October 1958, the improved Comet 4 series entered service.

Today, nearly all airliners are powered by jet engines. Thousands of jet engines, installed in hundreds of airliners, carry millions of passengers all over the world.

See also: AIRLINER.

Junk

A junk is a distinctive wooden-hulled sailing boat used extensively in the rivers and harbours of China as a lighter, along with the sampan. It may have from one to five masts, three being the average. The bow and stern are raised and blunt. Junks are often gaily painted in bright colours. Many Chinese families live aboard their junks permanently. There are also large sea-going junks.

Junks have special sails of bamboo matting or canvas, mounted on battens of wood set across the mast one below the other, rather like "Venetian blinds". This is one of their most distinctive features. Many now have diesel motors as well.

See also: SAMPAN.

Kayak

A kayak is an Eskimo canoe. The frame is made of bone (since there is little wood in Eskimo territory), and the covering is sealskin. The boat is completely decked over, with just a hole for the paddler to sit in. Once he has taken his place, he laces himself into the sealskin so tightly that, if

the kayak overturns, it does not fill with water. A sharp stroke of the Eskimo's paddle turns it right side up again. Kayaks range in size up to about twenty feet in length. They are fast, light and very seaworthy. Eskimos use them to hunt seals and walruses, for fishing and for travel.

See also: CANOE; UMIAK.

Land Yacht

This term is used here to describe the various forms of wheeled vehicles which, like the sailing boat, are driven by the wind.

Land yachts have never been successful as a means of transport because they cannot move without a strong wind blowing in the right direction, but sand-yachting is quite a popular sport.

See also: ICE YACHT.

Lift

A lift (known as an elevator in the United States of America) is a small compartment or platform used to raise or lower people or goods. Most lifts are installed in multi-storey buildings, but they are also used in the mining industry to carry miners to and from the coal face. Lifts usually operate inside shafts, but a few travel up and down the outside of buildings.

Until the invention of the lift the height of buildings was dictated by the number of stairs people were willing to climb. Five storeys was the usual limit. Skyscrapers would never have been practical if it had not been for the lift.

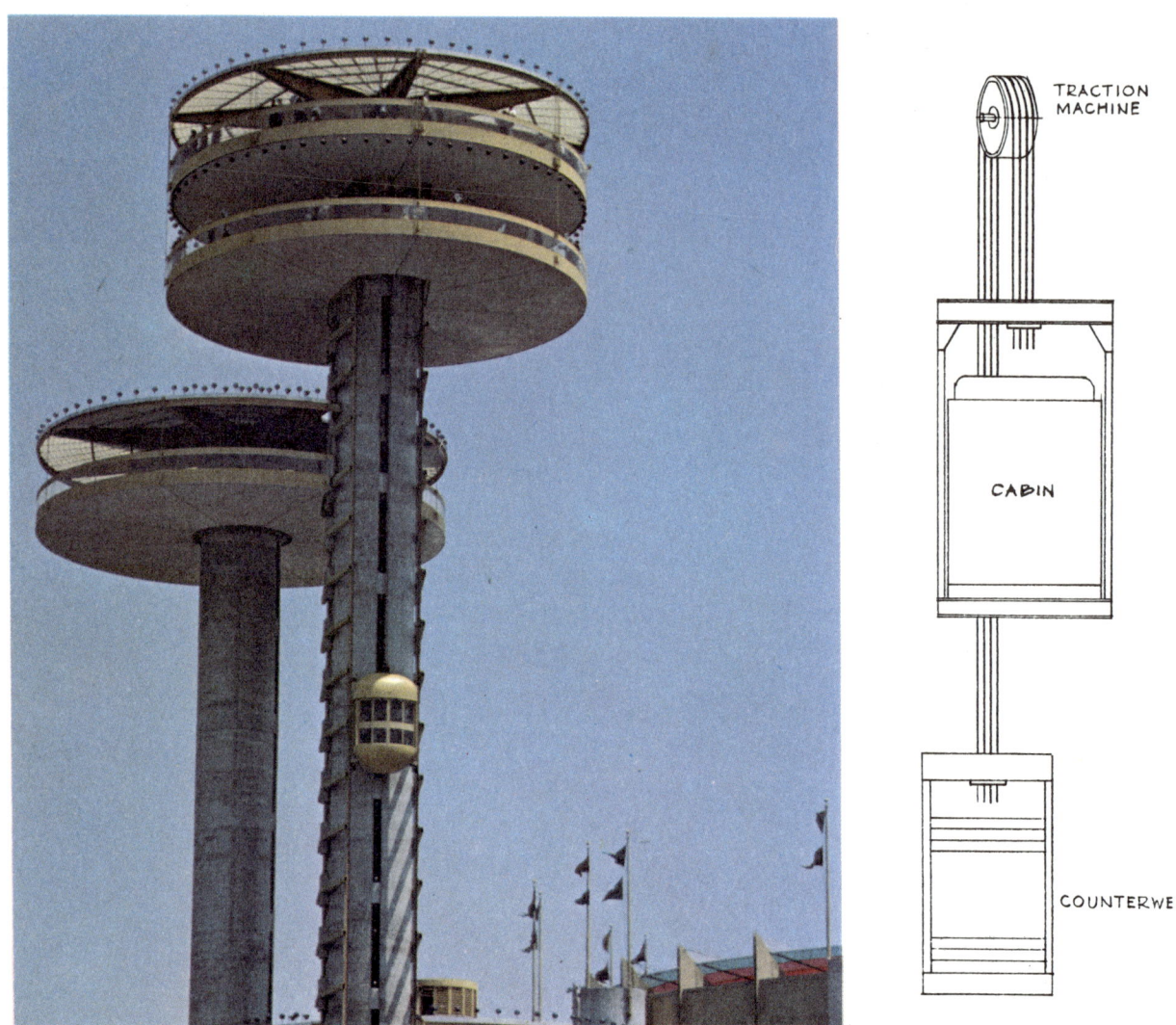

TRACTION MACHINE

CABIN

COUNTERWEIGHT

The first safe lift was invented in 1853 by Elisha G. Otis, an American. This was operated by steam and embodied a device that prevented the cabin from falling if the rope broke. In 1889, Otis installed the first electric lift in New York City.

A typical lift has a cabin running up and down in a shaft. Guide rails up the sides steady the cabin. An electric motor at the top is attached to pulleys. Steel cables attached to the top of the cabin pass round the pulleys and down to a heavy weight, known as the *counterweight*. This balances the weight of the cabin so that the motor does not have to haul the entire load.

Some lifts are run by operators, but most are self-service—that is, a passenger pushes a numbered button for the floor he wants, and the lift sets and stops automatically at that floor.

See also: PATERNOSTER.

60

Locomotive *See Diesel-electric Locomotive, Diesel-hydraulic Locomotive, Electric Locomotive, Steam Locomotive*

Lorry

Lorry is the general term applied to motor vehicles designed to carry freight and goods instead of people. Lorries (sometimes called trucks) are made in a wide variety of sizes and styles, many of which are intended for a special purpose. In this book "lorry" will also cover motor vans and other goods vehicles.

One of the most widely used is the simple, open, pick-up lorry, used for relatively light loads. It has an enclosed driver's cab in front and an open platform with sides at the rear. Somewhat similar is the van, on which the platform is covered in.

At the other extreme are the big, high-sided bulk haulage lorries used to transport coal, ore and other minerals.

Specialized lorries range from the softly-sprung vans used for transporting furniture to the refrigerated vans used to transport perishable foodstuffs.

Other specialized goods vehicles include the big tankers used to transport petrol, milk and bulk quantities of other liquids. Very specialized are the vehicles used to transport supercooled liquids such as liquid oxygen and hydrogen, and those used to transport cement. These cement carriers are easy to recognize by their distinctive cement "bucket", which rotates slowly, mixing the cement, while it is being carried to its destination.

Dumper, or tipper, trucks carry soil and rocks from building sites and during the construction of roads. These vehicles are made especially strong to withstand the very rough usage to which they are often subjected.

King of the motorways is the trailer truck, used to transport the large standardized containers in which an increasing proportion of goods is being carried.

Most impressive of all the road vehicles are the heavy-duty low loaders used to transport very heavy loads, such as electric transformers, weighing up to 200 tons, and other big pieces of machinery. These are often drawn by two power units, one pulling at the front and the other pushing at the rear.

See also: INTERNAL COMBUSTION ENGINE; MOTOR CAR.

REMOVAL VAN

PICK-UP LORRY

BOTTLE CARRIER

DUMPER TRUCK

SMALL VAN

PETROL TANKER

REFRIGERATED CONTAINER ON SEMI-TRAILER

LIVESTOCK LORRY

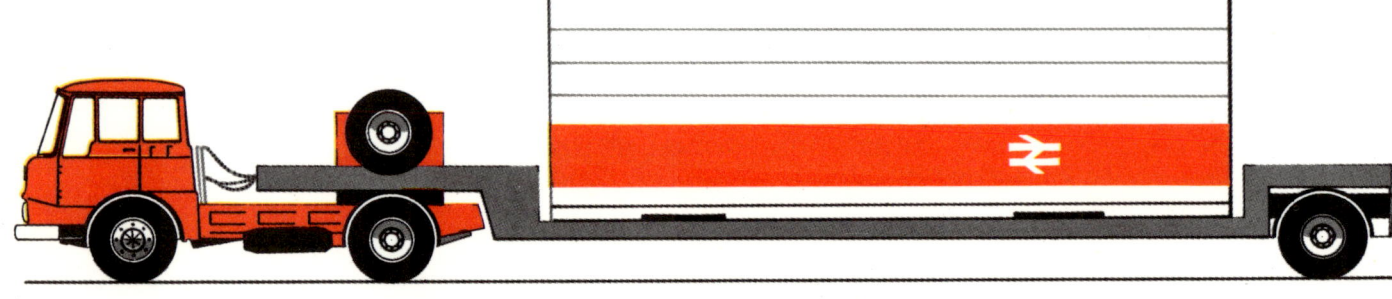

BRITISH RAIL CONTAINER ON LOW-LOAD SEMI-TRAILER

Lunar Roving Vehicle

This was used by the American Apollo 15 astronauts to explore the Moon. It has four wheels each of which is driven by its own electric motor. Power is supplied from two car-type batteries. The LRV has a maximum speed of 10 miles an hour.

An artist's impression of the Lunar Roving Vehicle

An unusual feature is the navigation system. This indicates the direction of the shortest distance back to the Lunar Module, so that the astronauts can return to it as quickly as possible if the vehicle breaks down or if some other emergency arises.

See also: LUNOKHOD; MODULAR EQUIPMENT TRANSPORTER.

Lunokhod

Lunokhod is an unmanned vehicle which was landed on the Moon in November 1970 by the Russians for the automatic exploration of the surface. The vehicle is driven by eight electrically-operated wheels. Power

is obtained by solar cell panels which convert the Sun's rays into electricity. Two television cameras mounted on the front enable controllers on Earth to see where the vehicle is going. Lunokhod transports a variety of scientific devices which test the consistency and make-up of the Moon's surface. Other equipment transmits the information back to the Earth.

See also: LUNAR ROVING VEHICLE; MODULAR EQUIPMENT TRANSPORTER.

Man

The first form of transport was man power. Man got from place to place on his own two feet. He carried burdens in his arms, on his back or on his head. He could travel at a rate of about 3 miles an hour. The amount of goods he could carry was limited by his strength. Later he developed back racks, harnesses and yokes to enable him to carry heavier loads over greater distances.

Two or more men were used to transport loads too heavy for one to carry. This was done by resting on their shoulder either a simple stick, from which the load was hung, or a stretcher-like frame on which the load was placed.

In modern society, both walking and carrying are common forms of transport. Most of us walk to school, carrying our books. We walk when we go shopping, and carry our purchases home. Ordinarily, of course, we do not transport heavy loads; for this we use machines. However, in many underdeveloped parts of the world, manpower is still more common than machines. In both India and China great roads and dams have been constructed, using men to transport the material required. In many parts of South and Central America, Asia and Africa, walking is still the chief means of land transport.

See also: PALANQUIN; SEDAN CHAIR.

Modular Equipment Transporter

This was a two-wheeled hand cart used by astronauts Alan Shepard and Edgar Mitchell during their expedition to the Moon in February, 1971, in the Apollo 14 spaceship *Antares*. The MET, as it was known for short, resembled a golf cart or tubular wheel-barrow, and was used to carry scientific equipment about the surface of the Moon.

See also: LUNOKHOD; LUNAR ROVING VEHICLE.

Monorail

Monorail is a railway on which the trains run on one track instead of two. The first monorail was opened in Ireland in 1888, since when semi-experimental tracks running over relatively short distances have been constructed on the mainland of Europe, in the United States and in Japan.

Monorails are usually raised in the air, thus minimizing the use of ground space and allowing other traffic to pass freely underneath. Most monorail carriages hang down underneath the supporting track, but some straddle it, the sides of the carriage hanging down to prevent it toppling over.

Monorails are unlikely to replace conventional two-track railways, as the single carriages usually carry fewer people. But they are useful in providing transport at large exhibitions and airports, and within cities.

See also: RAILWAY.

Motor Boat

The term motor boat covers any boat that is powered by a motor. Motor boats range in size and style from the tiniest runabout up to large yachts and fishing boats, or service boats such as police, fire and lifeboats.

The simplest type of motor boat is one with an *outboard* motor, that is, the motor is outside the hull. Most boats with outboard motors are small, but some cruisers of twenty feet or more, with bunks and cooking facilities, may be driven by such motors.

Inboard motor boats have motors inside their hulls. Sometimes the motor is at the rear, connected to the propeller by gears. Sometimes it is in the centre, connected to the propeller by a long propeller shaft. Both outboard and inboard motors are internal combustion engines.

Motor boats come in many styles. Small boats of ten to twenty feet are popular for weekend cruising in lakes and rivers, and for towing water-skiers. Small cabin cruisers are used by fishermen. Larger cabin cruisers with sleeping and cooking facilities are popular with people on holiday.

A *hydroplane* is a light motor boat with a very powerful engine. These fast boats skim over the surface of the water, and are often used for racing.

See also: HYDROFOIL; INTERNAL COMBUSTION ENGINE.

115 horse-power outboard motor boat

Motor Car

Until the motor car was invented, most vehicles were pulled along by horses or other animals. But the motor car has its own engine. It moves itself. So did the early steam-driven carriages, but these are so different from today's motor car, that they are described separately in this book.

Motor cars are so common today that it is hard for us to imagine life without any. But, less than a hundred years ago, the newfangled gadget was such a curiosity that one was featured in a circus.

The early history of the motor car is hard to trace, because there was no one inventor. Many people in many countries made contributions. Austria claims to have built the first car, the Marcus, made in 1875. Its ¼-horse-power engine had one cylinder and it had a top speed of 5 miles an hour. In 1879, Sedan, an American, built a petrol-driven car, but its engine had separate power and compression cylinders. It was very

inefficient. Five years later, using the now famous Otto four-stroke principle, Karl Benz produced a three-wheeled car with an engine.

However, the first real motor-car was a four-wheeled vehicle built by Gottlieb Daimler, a German engineer, in 1886. The engine developed 1½ horse-power and gave the car a top speed of 11 miles an hour.

Although considered the first motor car, the Daimler vehicle did not look like a present-day car. Like the vehicles which followed, it closely resembled a horse-drawn carriage—without, of course, the horses. The term "horseless carriage" was a good one for early motor cars.

Two Frenchmen, Panhard and Levassor, are credited with making the first motor car with everything in the right place. They mounted the engine at the front, under a bonnet. The drive was taken to the back wheels by a friction clutch, controlled by a foot-pedal. Speed was changed by a "gear-box", although the gears were not actually boxed in.

In Britain, unfortunately, development was almost at a standstill

Milburn light electric brougham, 1910　　　　*Packard runabout, 1908*

owing to the notorious "Red Flag Act". In 1865 this had been passed at the instigation of the owners of horse-drawn vehicles to curtail the growing popularity of steam-driven carriages. The law required that every road vehicle must have a crew of three, including one person to walk in front carrying a red flag. The maximum speed permitted was 4 miles an hour. When the act became law, progress in Britain virtually stopped.

Things did not improve until the act was repealed in 1896. To celebrate the event, fifty-four cars took part in a London-to-Brighton run—an event which is still commemorated by an annual run in November. Most of the cars taking part in the original run were foreign—and represented nearly all the cars in the whole of Britain at that time!

With the repeal of the act, British engineers began to make up for lost time. Cleverest of the early designers was Dr F. W. Lanchester. He produced original designs and his vehicles are considered to be the first truly British cars.

In addition to petrol-driven cars, a number of people built electric cars. Their power came from large batteries, and they were quiet and clean. But they were not very fast and after travelling about fifty miles the battery

Ford "Model T" touring car, 1910　　　　*Stanley Steam touring car, 1911*

Rolls-Royce "Silver Ghost", 1912

Austin touring car, 1913

was dead. Changing it or recharging it was troublesome. The electric car went out of favour in 1910, and today their use is confined to small delivery vehicles that have to make frequent stops, such as milk floats. However, there is hope that one day the invention of a new form of battery may make the small electric car practical and economical.

As far as petrol-driven cars are concerned, events which were to make motoring possible for the average person were taking place in the United States. In that country a remarkable young man was determined to make a car that was not only reliable, but cheap. The man's name was Henry Ford.

At first Ford built cars like everyone else did in those days, like a house, in one place. The chassis was the foundation; it stood in one spot and was not moved until it was finished by the addition of the engine, radiator, wheels, wings, seats and doors. It was a laborious process.

Ford changed all this by copying a scheme developed nearly one hundred years previously, when the government wanted 10,000 muskets quickly. The various parts were all made so accurately that the job of assembling a complete gun was a simple matter of joining any of the pieces

"Bullnose" Morris Oxford, 1926

Bentley "Speed 6", 1930

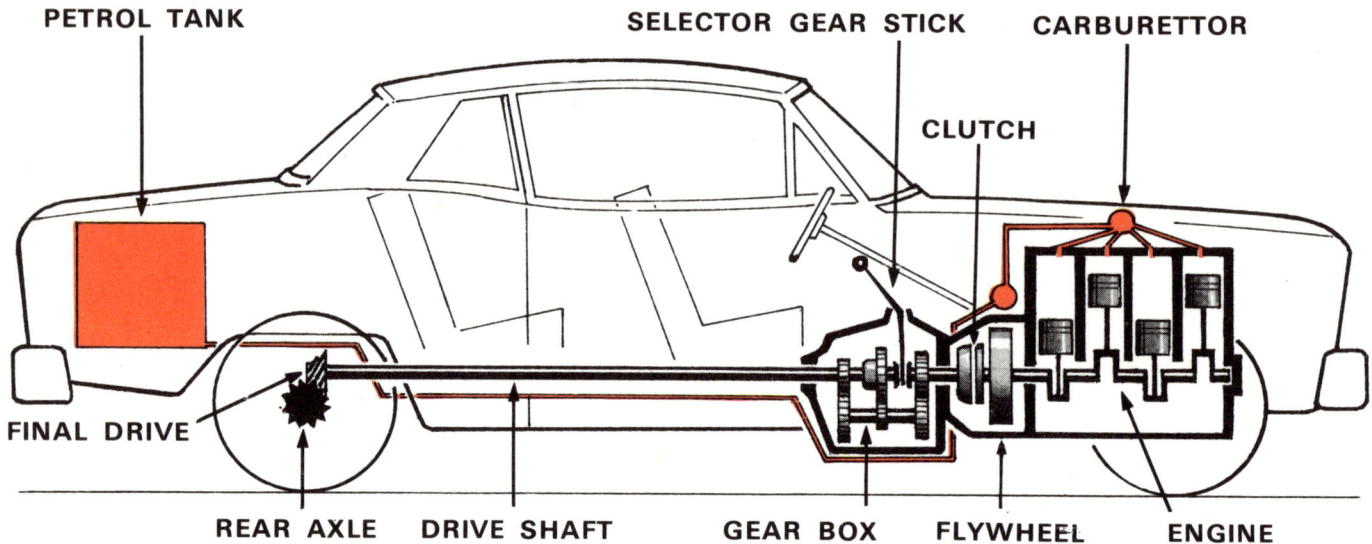

PETROL TANK   SELECTOR GEAR STICK   CARBURETTOR

CLUTCH

FINAL DRIVE

REAR AXLE   DRIVE SHAFT   GEAR BOX   FLYWHEEL   ENGINE

together. Ford used the idea and designed machines to make the various parts exactly alike, so that any one was interchangeable with the other. Ford also developed the idea of the conveyor belt system to move the various parts to the workers, to save time. On the first assembly line, the chassis were pulled along by a rope. This simple idea cut the time for assembling a car from twelve hours to less than six.

Then the production line was mechanized, and the production of Ford Model Ts went up and up. At first Ford had dreamed of building a car every minute—but soon a car was coming off the production line every ten seconds. During one incredible day in 1925, over 9,000 cars were made in twenty-four hours.

The appearance of the Ford Model T, and of the hundreds of other makes of car which followed it, revolutionized people's way of life all over the world. For the first time a vehicle was available for ordinary people which gave them a mobility far beyond the dreams of the rich and the noble of earlier ages. People began to move about much more, both for pleasure and in travelling to and from work.

Some other British pioneers of the motor car whose names are still well-known because of the cars that bear their names were Charles S. Rolls, Henry Royce and William Morris. Today the manufacture of motor cars in countries such as the United States, Britain, France, Germany, Sweden, Japan and Italy is of vital importance to the prosperity of these countries.

We live in the age of the motor car. It is, perhaps, the most important and most widely used form of transport in the world. About one hundred million are in daily use throughout the world.

See also: INTERNAL COMBUSTION ENGINE; LORRY; STEAM CARRIAGE.

Motor Cycle

A motor cycle (often called a motor bike) is a two-wheeled vehicle powered by a small petrol engine. It is usually ridden by one person, but most have a seat behind the driver for a passenger as well. Some motor cycles have a third wheel and a sidecar, for an extra passenger. These motor cycles are called combinations.

Daimler's first motor cycle

The motor cycle was developed from the bicycle. Daimler developed a small petrol engine in 1885 which he attached to a bicycle for testing, and thus unwittingly invented the motor cycle. From that time on the motor cycle developed quickly.

Today, the motor cycle has a heavy frame, with the engine mounted in the centre, between the wheels. A kick-starter turns over the engine. The

accelerator, which controls the speed, is on the handlebars. So is the front-wheel brake and the clutch. The rear-wheel brake and gears are operated by means of foot pedals.

Motor cycles are used for both transport and sport. They are also popular with town police, as they can move between cars in heavy traffic.

See also: INTERNAL COMBUSTION ENGINE.

Motor Scooter

A motor scooter is similar to a motor cycle, but is smaller and with a lighter frame and engine. The wheels are usually smaller than those of a motor cycle, and the engine, instead of being placed between the wheels, is either above or just in front of the rear wheel.

The frame is less bicycle-like, the rider's feet resting on a small floor.

Motor scooters are particularly popular in Britain and Europe, where they provide fast, cheap transport. The distinctive *putt-putt* of their engines is a familiar sound in cities.

See also: INTERNAL COMBUSTION ENGINE.

Moving Pavement

A moving pavement at a big international airport

A moving pavement is just what its name says it is—a pavement that moves. It is a conveyor belt for people. Moving pavements are used in areas where there are large crowds in a hurry. Thus they are used at many airports, for example, at Heathrow Airport, where one of them carries travellers up the long corridor joining the main terminal building with the jumbo-jet lounges at the other end. To move even faster passengers can walk along the moving pavement.

Similar to a moving pavement is the *travelator* at the Bank station of the London Underground. This is actually a moving ramp as it is on a gentle slope.

See also: ESCALATOR.

Nuclear Ship

Just as the steamship replaced the sailing ship, so some day the nuclear ship may replace the conventional coal or oil-fired ship. The nuclear has one big advantage over all other kinds of powered vessel. The heat required to generate the steam to operate the turbines driving the propellers is produced from an atomic, or nuclear, reactor; this means a nuclear ship can travel long distances on a small quantity of fuel.

The first nuclear merchant ship was the American *Savannah*, which went into service in 1962. The ship was named after the old steam-sailing ship *Savannah*, which set out to cross the Atlantic under steam in 1819, ran out of fuel and completed the journey under sail. There will be no such problem on the new *Savannah*, for she can travel round the world twelve times on 700 pounds of uranium fuel.

The *Savannah* looks much like any ordinary coal or oil-fired ship, except that there are no funnels. This is because there is no fire making smoke. The ship is about 600 feet long and has a crew of 110. She can carry 60 passengers and 10,000 tons of cargo.

In 1964 West Germany put the nuclear ship *Otto Hahn* into service. Russia has nuclear-powered ice-breakers in service.

See also: SHIP; STEAMSHIP; SUBMARINE.

Palanquin

The palanquin, an early form of transport for one passenger, was used in India and China and consisted of a box-like compartment supported on two long poles. Four men, two in front and two behind, used the poles to lift and carry the palanquin. The sides of the compartment were simply shutters or blinds which could be opened by the passenger.

See also: MAN; SEDAN CHAIR.

Paternoster

This is a special kind of lift and consists of a ring of cars, arranged like a string of beads, which operates continuously. One side of the "string" goes up and the other side goes down, the line of cars being guided round curved rails at the top and bottom. There are no doors, as on normal lifts, and passengers just step into the first empty car which comes into view. The cars remain upright all the time so that passengers who forget to get off at the top or bottom floors do not reappear upside down!

Entry into and exit from a car on the move is a little frightening at first, but soon becomes second nature. Paternosters are usually installed in hospitals or busy office buildings, where there is continuous movement of staff between floors.

See also: LIFT.

Pedicab

The pedicab is the taxi cab of the Orient. It is basically a three-wheeled cart, with a passenger seat located between the two front wheels. It is propelled by foot pedals, like a bicycle. Pedicabs are as common in many cities in the Far East as taxis are in London and New York.

See also: RICKSHAW.

Pipeline

More than two thousand years ago the Chinese used hollow bamboo stalks to transport water. The archaeologists who dug up the ancient Roman city of Pompeii found lead pipes buried in the ground. The first pipeline in the United States was made of bored-out logs. It was in Fredonia, New York, and was used to transport natural gas.

The first iron pipeline was built in 1865 by Samuel Van Syckel to carry oil from his well in Pennsylvania to a railway five miles away. The cast-iron pipe was two inches across and it leaked at the joints. Even so, it carried 800 barrels of oil a day.

Today, North America alone has over a million miles of pipeline—four times the distance to the Moon. The growth of pipelines in many other parts of the world has also been spectacular. Some pipes are more than a yard in diameter. Pumps all along the routes of the pipelines keep the oil (or whatever the pipe is carrying) flowing quickly and smoothly.

In addition to crude oil and natural gas, pipelines carry diesel fuel, petrol, paraffin, and other petroleum products. Rather surprisingly, pipelines are also used to transport solids such as coal, minerals, sand, gravel and metals! The solids are put into the pipelines with a liquid and are carried along in the stream. When it is necessary to protect the solids they are sealed in plastic bags or capsules.

Two of the biggest pipelines in the world are the *Big Inch* and the *Little Big Inch* in the United States. They carry natural gas and petroleum products and both start in Texas and run eastwards. The *Big Inch* runs for 1,341 miles and the *Little Big Inch* for 1,475. Another pipeline, 2,900 miles long, carries natural gas from Texas to New York City.

For the past few years a small army of men and machines has been busy criss-crossing Britain with a network of pipelines to distribute the natural gas discovered under the North Sea. The work of burying the pipes is likely to continue for several years yet.

Pipelines are sometimes laid on top of the ground and sometimes buried to depths of 200 feet or more. They can cross rivers, lakes, mountains and deserts. Weather or traffic cannot harm them. Sometimes the pipes develop leaks, and trouble-shooters in aeroplanes and helicopters are constantly on the lookout for these. It is easy to spot a natural gas leak from the air, because the nearby grass and leaves turn yellow.

Another way to check what is happening inside a pipeline is to add a bit of radioactive material to the product. Checkers along the route with the help of Geiger counters can tell immediately where a blockage has occurred.

It is possible to send many different products through a pipeline simultaneously, one after the other. A radioactive isotope tells when one product has passed and another is about to arrive. This is the signal to open and close the right valves so that the product in the pipeline is routed correctly. For instance, crude oil may go straight to a refinery, paraffin to another kind of factory and petrol to a tanker or a railway.

One of the great engineering feats of modern times is the *European Transalpine Pipeline*. It runs from the tanker docks in Trieste, Italy, across the Austrian Alps, to oil refineries in West Germany. Twelve international companies co-operated to build the pipeline, which is 288 miles long. It transports 40 million tons of oil a year.

Pony Express

The Pony Express was started in 1860 to provide quick mail service across America. The route ran between St. Joseph, Missouri, and Sacramento, California.

A rider with his bag of mail left the first station and galloped on horseback as fast as he could to the next station, ten or fifteen miles away. There, a fresh horse waited, saddled and ready to go.

Every fifty miles the mail was turned over to a new rider who continued the journey.

The Pony Express used 400 horses and 125 riders. It covered the 1,900-mile route in eight days.

Raft

A raft is a simple platform which floats on water. It usually drifts with the current, but can be powered by paddles, poles or sails.

Early man's first boat was a raft, made of logs or reeds lashed together with vines. During the eighteenth century, large wooden rafts called *flatboats* were an important means of transport on the Mississippi and Ohio Rivers, in the United States. The early pioneers heading west piled furniture, family and livestock on the rafts. There was a small hut-like enclosure in the centre for privacy and shelter.

Modern rafts are usually small wooden platforms often floated on empty oil drums and anchored in swimming areas. Swimmers also use blown-up rafts of rubber or plastic. Rubber rafts are also used as life rafts for boats, aircraft and spacecraft.

In 1947, Thor Heyerdahl, a Norwegian scientist, built a raft of balsa wood. Heyerdahl and five companions drifted from Peru to the Tuamotu Islands in the Pacific, a distance of over 4,000 miles. He copied the design of the rafts used by the ancient Polynesians, and he named his raft *Kon-Tiki* after an old Polynesian god.

Railway

George Stephenson's ROCKET

The first passenger railway was opened in 1825. It ran from Stockton-on-Tees to Darlington. The locomotive was George Stephenson's *Loco-motion No. 1*, and it pulled 34 wagons carrying about 600 passengers at an average speed of 6 miles an hour. There was a band on board to entertain the passengers and a man on horseback rode in front of the train waving a red flag to warn people of the coming of the train. Soon after it was opened, however, the line went back to pulling its trains by horses!

It was not until five years later that the first regular steam railway opened, running between Liverpool and Manchester. In 1829 a competition for locomotives was held by the directors of the railway, as some of them thought the new line ought to be operated by horses, and others thought fixed engines and cables would be best. George Stephenson, who had built the track, naturally wanted them to use a steam locomotive and entered his new *Rocket*. This engine had copper tubes passing from the fire box through the boiler, and out of the smoke-stack. In this way the water was heated much more quickly and the engine travelled faster than any Stephenson had yet built. Also, the wheels were driven directly from the cylinders.

For the competition each locomotive had to run twenty times in each direction, pulling a train three times its own weight. Of the five engines entered, only the *Rocket* successfully fulfilled all the conditions, completing the 60 miles at an average speed of 14 miles an hour, and completing the last lap at 29 miles an hour.

A year later the Liverpool and Manchester line was opened and, because of the success of the *Rocket*, became the first entirely locomotive-

Peter Cooper's TOM THUMB

worked line in the world. It embodied all kinds of improvements such as tunnels, bridges, double tracks, signals and stations.

The triumph of the railway did not discourage its enemies, and genuinely frightened many people. At first cattle were disturbed by trains, and farmers feared that sparks from the chimney would set fire to the crops. In Parliament, learned men argued that people would not be able to withstand the unnatural speed of trains. One person suggested, in the interests of safety, that on each journey the locomotive should carry two directors of the railway company—tied to the boiler! Teachers even taught children how to travel in a train with the least possible danger. In spite of such opposition, railways continued to be built everywhere, not only in Britain but in Europe and North and South America as well.

At the same time, the railway arrived in the New World. A British-

A doubleheaded passenger train in the United States, 1885

built locomotive, the *Stourbridge Lion*, began to haul a train from Carbondale to Honesdale, Pennsylvania, in 1829.

As in Britain, there were many people in America who laughed at the new railway and who said it would never replace the horse. To answer them Peter Cooper of New York built a tiny locomotive in 1830. He called it *Tom Thumb* and raced it against a horse-drawn carriage. For a time the *Tom Thumb* was in the lead but, suddenly, something broke, and it came to a stop. In this instance the horse won, but in other similar races the "iron horses" won. Little by little it became clear that the railway was here to stay.

In 1830, the Baltimore and Ohio and South Carolina railways opened a few miles of track for regular passenger runs. Five years later there were a thousand miles of track in use and two hundred lines had been planned or were under construction in eleven different states.

Railways were springing up in Europe too. France, Italy, Belgium,

Germany, Holland, Austria, Switzerland, Denmark and Spain, all had railways by 1850. Soon railways were spanning whole continents.

In the United States, by 1858, the railways had expanded enormously. The gold rush in 1849 opened up the West, and as settlers moved westwards so did the railways. A line from east to west was started, but work was interrupted by the Civil War. After the war, the track was completed. The Union Pacific Railroad Company, starting in the east and stretching westwards, and the Central Pacific Railroad Company starting from Sacramento, California, raced towards each other. Thousands of workers toiled through the deserts, mountains and wilderness, fighting off attacks by Indians. At last, on 10th May, 1896, the two tracks met at Promontory, Utah. There, as a locomotive stood at each end of the track, the final section was laid and fixed with a ceremonial golden spike. This historic link of east and west was followed within a few years by several other transcontinental lines.

The importance of railways cannot be over-emphasized. By carrying passengers swiftly and transporting enormous quantities of freight, railways helped to unify countries. For example, in 1835, Germany consisted of not less than 38 different small states. By 1870, however, a great network of 10,000 miles of railways had been built, enabling letters, documents and people to travel quickly to remote towns and villages. Germany for the first time in its history, became one nation.

The World War of 1914–18 also showed the efficiency of railways. The speed of armies was greatly increased by using railways and motor-powered road vehicles. From earliest times to Napoleon, columns of troops could move only as fast as a man on foot. Even with the horse-drawn wagon, then the only known vehicle, armies could move only at walking pace. There was no way of moving vast numbers of soldiers quickly.

The historic meeting of the Union Pacific and Central Pacific Railroads at Promontory, Utah

Railways solved this problem. Their large capacity was ideal for the transport of troops. Armies could now move at the speed of a locomotive. It was a speed that, only a hundred years before, not even the most optimistic engineer or general had ever dreamed of.

In Europe the transcontinental lines included the famous Orient Express from Paris to Istanbul, and the great Trans-Siberian railway, from Moscow to Vladivostok, which is the longest in the world—5,787 miles.

Today, there are more than a million miles of line spanning the world—enough rail to go round the globe forty times.

All early railways used steam locomotives. Although these had power and speed, they were inconvenient, dirty, wasteful and expensive—using up both fuel and water while waiting at a station or siding.

Engineers began to consider using electricity. Initially, battery-powered locomotives were built, but none was successful. The end of the nineteenth century saw the birth of electric traction. Development of electrification in Britain, up to 1914, was based on D.C. (direct current) supply, using a third rail.

Nowadays, however, British Rail uses A.C. (alternating current) at a high voltage (25,000 volts) which is fed to the trains through overhead wires.

At the same time British Rail developed locomotives with diesel engines. Today nearly all locomotives are diesel-electrics, that is the diesel engine is used to operate a generator which produces electricity to drive its wheels. Such locomotives are cleaner and more efficient than steam locomotives, and have a rapid acceleration.

Britain combined the two forms of traction, using electricity on lines with the highest traffic density and diesel on main and other branch lines. However most main lines are now being electrified.

The expansion of air travel facilities and the construction of motorways has had an adverse effect on the railway systems in many countries. For example, fewer people now travel across the United States, or from Moscow to Vladivostok, by train. People go by air which is not only much quicker but, in the United States, sometimes cheaper too. The development of motorways and the increasing use of the motor car has led to so few passengers using some country lines that they have had to be

BRITISH RAIL ROLLING STOCK

TIPPER WAGON

BRAKE VAN

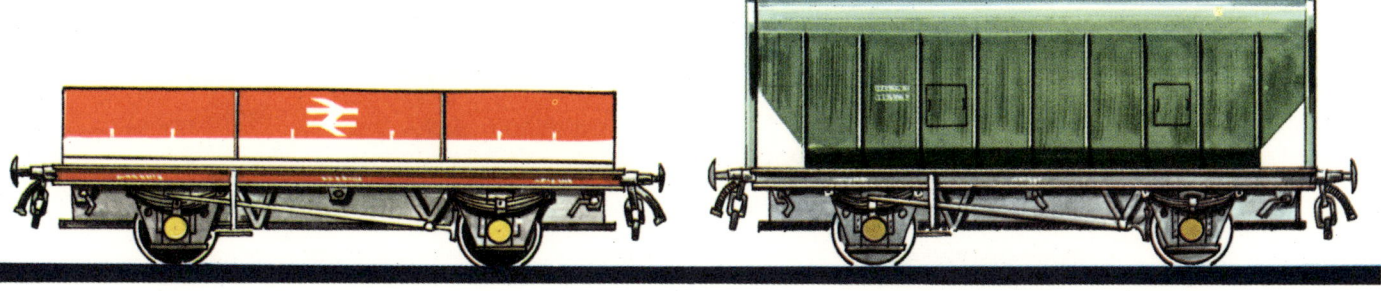

HALF-CAR

BULK GRAIN WAGON

CLASS 75 1,250 H.P. DIESEL LOCOMOTIVE

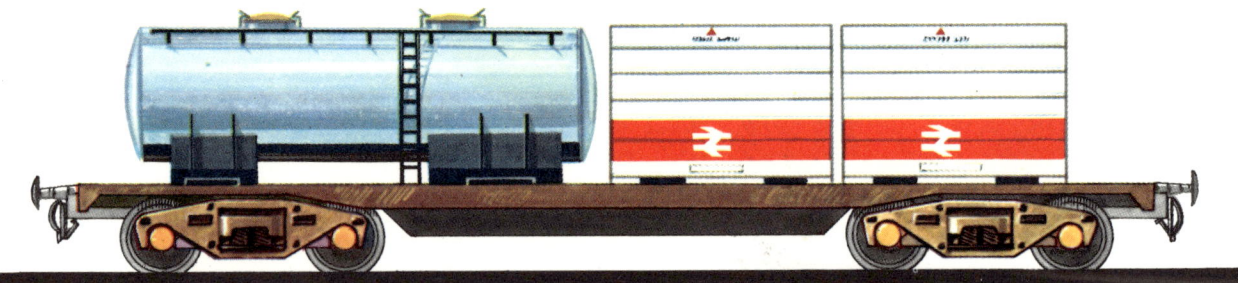

FLAT CAR—COMBINED ROAD–RAIL AND TANKER CONTAINERS

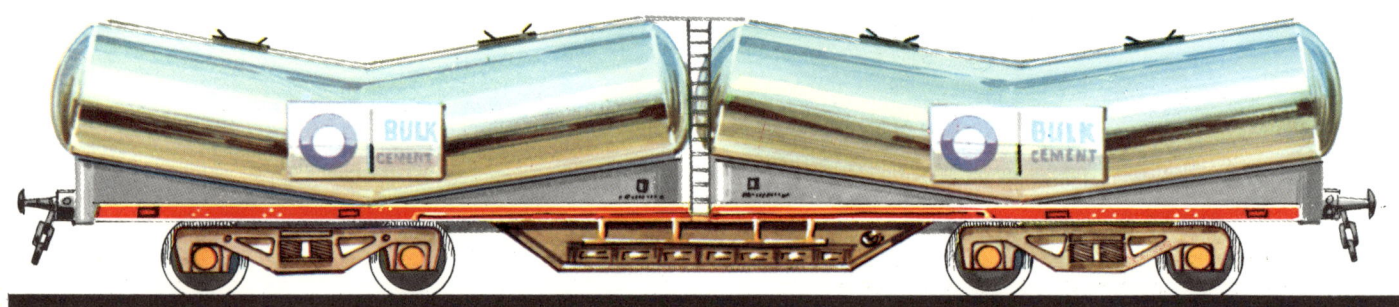

100-TON CAPACITY BULK CEMENT TANKERS

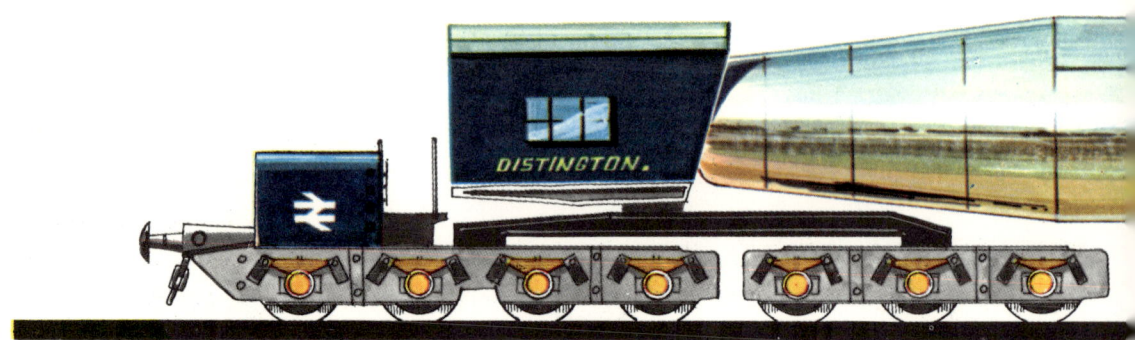

100-TON CAPACITY MOLT

CATTLE WAGON   COAL HOPPER

HIGHLY-INSULATED REFRIGERATED CONTAINER

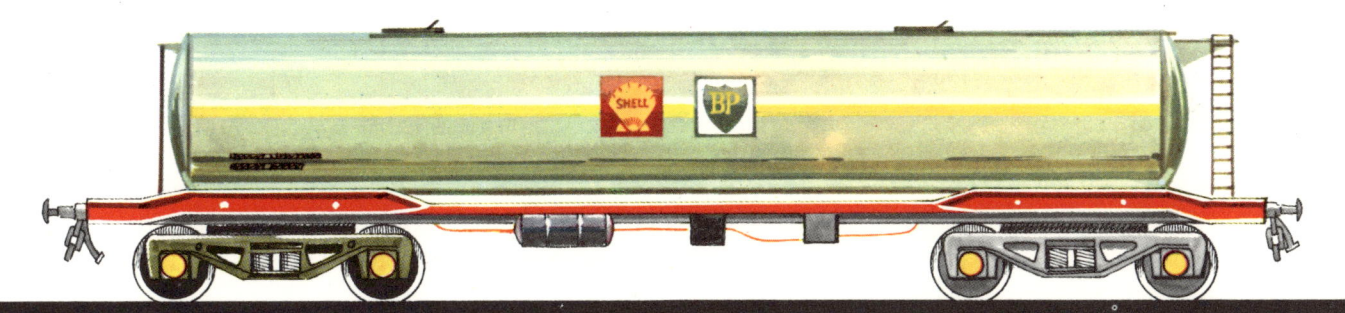

21,000-GALLON CAPACITY PETROL TANKER

TEEL CARRIER (TORPEDO WAGON)

The GOLDEN ARROW *boat train which runs between London and Dover*

closed. Road transport being able to deliver direct to the destination has also taken much freight trade away from railways.

Railways, however, still provide the best means of transporting bulk freight, such as coal and minerals. Also, better and faster trains are being developed to attract passengers away from air travel, at least over short distances.

Most main-line passenger trains in Britain average 80 miles an hour, and special trains in France, Italy and Japan average over 100 miles an hour. The fastest scheduled train, in Japan, averages 135 miles an hour. In France test speeds of over 200 miles an hour have been achieved.

In Britain a new high-speed diesel-electric train is being built, which is designed to average 125 miles an hour on long runs. Even faster will be the Advanced Passenger Train powered by a gas-turbine engine. This will embody revolutionary stabilizing equipment, enabling the train to take curves safely at high speed.

See also: ELECTRIC LOCOMOTIVE; DIESEL-ELECTRIC LOCOMOTIVE; DIESEL-HYDRAULIC LOCOMOTIVE; MONORAIL; STEAM LOCOMOTIVE; UNDERGROUND.

The FLYING SCOTSMAN *which travels between London and Edinburgh*

Rickshaw

The rickshaw, or *jinricksha*, was introduced in Japan about 1869 and was once the taxicab of the Orient. In China, Japan and some other countries, men did the work of horses between the shafts of a two-wheeled cart. The passengers sat in the cart and the runner, or *hiki*, bent between the shafts pulled them along. Hikis commonly covered twenty to thirty miles a day and earned barely enough money to stay alive.

Rickshaws have been outlawed in most places and have been replaced by pedicabs.

See also: PEDICAB.

Rocket Belt

This is a small rocket engine which is strapped to the back of the wearer. The rocket points downwards, so that when it is started, the wearer is lifted straight up. The rocket can lift a man over a hundred feet up in the air and carry him a quarter of a mile.

The rocket belt can be used to lift troops across rivers or other obstacles. It could also be used for rescue operations: for example, to rescue a climber who may be injured and stranded high up on a mountain.

Roller Skates

Roller skates are not an important means of transport. They are used chiefly for sport and by children for pleasure, although one or two people have skated to work when their ordinary means of transport has not been available.

Roller skates for outside use have steel, ball-bearing wheels. The platform of the skate clamps on to the shoe and a leather strap fastens round the ankle.

For indoor skating on a rink, roller skates are often attached to their own shoes and have wood, plastic or rubber wheels.

The first roller skates were invented by Joseph Merlin of London in 1760.

Rowing Boat

A rowing boat is a boat that is propelled by one or more persons using oars. The most common kind of rowing boat is rowed by only one

Single sculls

Eight-man racing crew

person. He uses two oars, one on each side, the oars being held in place by rowlocks.

Rowing boats were in use as early as 3000 B.C. The ancient Greeks, Romans and Vikings all used huge rowing boats with many rowers. These boats also often had sails.

Today, in addition to pleasure rowing on lakes and rivers, there is much interest in racing. In *scull* racing, each rower uses two oars. The number of crew varies from one to eight.

In *sweep-oar* racing, each rower uses a single oar. Boats for these races are designed for two, four, six or eight oarsmen. Britain's most famous rowing events are the Oxford–Cambridge Boat Race and the Henley Regatta.

See also: GALLEY.

Sailing Ships and Boats

At one time wooden sailing ships ruled the seas. They carried goods and people across the great oceans which cover most of the surface of the Earth. Today their work is done by steel ships, powered by steam or diesel engines, and by aircraft. The age of the big sailing ship for commercial use has gone for ever.

Today, however, sailing is a popular sport and sailing boats are used throughout the world mostly for pleasure.

The smallest sailing boats, called dinghies, are only about eight feet long. The boat often comes in a kit so that the owner can put it together himself. Relatively small sailing boats have travelled round the world.

The body of the boat is the *hull*. Reaching into the water along the hull is either a *keel*, which remains in place, or a *centreboard* which can be raised and lowered. These keep the boat from sliding sideways or tipping over when the wind pushes against the sails.

The *rudder* goes down into the water from the stern of the boat and is used to steer it. On a small sailing boat, the rudder is moved with a handle called a *tiller*. A large boat has a *wheel*.

A *spar* is any pole that holds a sail. The upright spars are the *masts*. The largest sail is on the *mainmast*. There may be a *mizzenmast* towards the stern or a *foremast* towards the bow. Both of these are shorter than the mainmast.

A *boom* or a *gaff* is a pole that is fastened at right angles to a mast. It holds the sails out straight—the boom at the bottom, the gaff at the top.

The *mainsail* is exactly that—the main sail. A smaller, triangular sail in front of the mainsail is a *jib*. A large jib that reaches behind the

BRIG

CAT

BRIGANTINE

KETCH

YAWL

LUGGER

BARKENTINE

BARK

CLIPPER

SLOOP

SCHOONER

95

mainmast is called a *Genoa jib*. A *spinnaker* is a large parachute-like sail that adds a great deal of speed as it balloons with air where there is an almost directly following wind.

Rigging means all the ropes and lines. *Standing rigging* holds the masts steady. It is never taken down. *Running rigging* is attached to the sails and booms. The lines that make the sails go up or down are the *halyards*. The lines that adjust or *trim* the sails are *sheets*.

There are different ways of arranging the sails and masts on a sailing boat and this is called the way the boat is *rigged*. Most pleasure and racing boats are *fore-and-aft rigged* with one large triangular sail behind the mast and a smaller one in front. One end of the boom is attached to the mast. It holds the sail straight out behind the mast.

Most sailing ships of the Middle Ages were *square-rigged*, that is the sails did not run fore and aft, but *across* the ships from side to side. These sails had four sides and were not held out by booms or gaffs. Instead, they were fastened on long spars called *yards* and hung at their centres from the mast. The *Pamir* was the last of the square-rigged ships to carry a cargo. She was lost in 1957, 500 miles south of the Azores.

Each kind of sailing ship has its own name, depending on its size and rig. Some of the different types are shown on page 95.

Primitive people knew how to make sailing boats. As long as they were willing to go the way the wind was blowing, there was no problem. They just got blown along. As they grew more skilful, they learned that they could go in other directions, too. A sailing boat cannot go right against the wind, but it can zigzag back and forth. This is called *tacking*. A sailing boat can also sail across the wind and this is called *reaching*. Sailing before the wind (with the wind behind you) is *running*.

Sailing requires a good deal of practice and skill. Small sailing boats can turn over easily and you should never go out in one without a life jacket.

See also: BOAT; CLIPPER SHIP; GALLEON; ICE YACHT; JUNK; SCHOONER; SHIP; WARSHIP; YACHT.

Sampan

A sampan is a small open boat used in the rivers and harbours of China and Japan. It is propelled by an oar and often carries a sail as well.

A distinctive feature is the small cabin of straw matting. Sampans are often used as homes.

See also: JUNK.

Schooner

A schooner under full sail

A schooner was a sailing ship rigged with fore-and-aft sails. It had usually two or three masts, although there were some with five or six masts. Schooners with seven masts have been known. Schooners are relatively rare now, but are still quite common in the Pacific islands, the Caribbean and the Mediterranean. At one time, they were very popular as cargo ships, particularly in coastal waters.

One of the first schooners was built by Andrew Robinson at Gloucester, Massachusetts, in 1713. The legend is that as the ship was launched a spectator cried out, "There she scoons!" *Scoon* is a New England dialect word which means to skim along the water. Somehow the word stuck to the ship, although the spelling was changed to schooner.

See also: CLIPPER SHIP; SAILING SHIPS AND BOATS.

Sedan Chair

A sedan chair is a portable chair or compartment, usually borne on poles by two men, and holding only one person. The outsides of the compartment and the carrying poles were often beautifully decorated.

Sedan chairs were extremely popular in Europe during the eighteenth century, especially in London and Paris. The chair was introduced into England in 1634 and is said to have been first used in the French town of Sedan. Chairs of similar design had been known long before, the most famous being the ancient *sedia gestatoria* used by the popes in Rome.

See also: MAN; PALANQUIN.

Ship

A ship is a large sea-going vessel. To be called a ship a vessel may not be propelled by oars or paddles, but this was not always the case. Nowadays a ship is the general term applied to vessels from about 100 feet in length and of 300 tons in weight to the largest passenger liners, bulk cargo carriers and warships.

The earliest ships were very crude. They may have been nothing more than a hollowed-out log or a bundle of logs, hardly more than a raft. A modern passenger liner is a floating city. It generates its own heat and electricity and has many cabins and shops.

The history of ships is a long one. No one knows when the first ships were built, but it was thousands of years ago. By 1500 B.C. the Egyptians had taken to the sea in wooden ships that were as much as 70 feet long. They had one sail and a number of oars on each side. The Egyptians often carved the front of their ships in the shape of swans or ducks.

From about 1000 B.C. until the time of Christ, the chief sailors of the Mediterranean were the Phoenicians. Their ships were called *galleys*. Sometimes they had two, or even three, rows of oars, one above the other, on each side.

The ancient Greeks also had galleys. They were long and narrow. They were used chiefly as warships and had to be very fast and manoeuvrable.

Not all Greek ships were warships; some of their vessels carried on trade between the islands of the Mediterranean. Trading ships got most of their power from sails and were blunter in shape than the long war

PHOENICIAN GALLEY   DUGOUT CANOE

LOG

galleys. Since they were not used for fighting, they were built for sturdiness and cargo space rather than speed.

The ancient Romans also used a combination of sails and oars for their war galleys. The oarsmen were usually slaves and were known as *galley slaves*.

The Vikings, too, were great early sailors. From about A.D. 750 until the twelfth century their ships travelled the North Atlantic, the Baltic Sea, and even the Mediterranean. Viking ships were usually open and flat-bottomed with a beautifully shaped hull sweeping up to a great carved figurehead at the bow. They had one sail and a number of oars.

The one-sail, or one-masted, ship remained in use until long after the Crusades (1095–1192). By about 1400, sailors had begun to add an extra sail, called a *lateen sail*, to aid steering. This sail was triangular and hung from a *mizzenmast*. The large square sail hung from the *mainmast*. The sailors soon found that they could go faster if they added another square sail on a *foremast*. Different arrangements of square and lateen sails were tried. Paintings of Columbus's ships show the sails arranged in different ways. Such ships were rather light and fast and were known as *caravels*.

During the 1500s, the Spanish *galleon* became the chief ship of Europe. It was larger than a caravel and usually well armed. More of the ship was enclosed to provide protected quarters for the crew. Extra decks were

MEDIEVAL ROUND SHIP

VIKING *DRAKKAR*

added. The biggest advances in sailing ships were made in the 1800s with the *clipper ship* and the *windjammer*.

By the mid-nineteenth century the sailing ship began gradually to be replaced by vessels deriving power from steam engines, although for some time vessels continued to be powered by both sail and steam. The new steamships were propelled by paddles. Later they were propelled by the screw propeller, invented by John Ericsson and Francis Pettit Smith. Hulls began to be made of iron instead of wood. The last wooden warship, *Repulse*, was launched in 1868.

The first real iron ship was the *Vulcan*, a British sailing ship built in 1818. It was followed by a British steamship, *Aaron Manby*, which was launched in 1821.

Towards the end of the nineteenth century the replacement of iron by steel was the next great step forward in shipbuilding. The first steel merchant ship of any size was the *Rotomahana*, built by Denny on the Clyde.

In 1894, the steam turbine, which today provides power for most of the world's great liners, was introduced by Sir Charles Parsons on the *Turbinia*. In 1897 she achieved the speed of 34 knots!

Improved hull construction kept pace with greater engine power, and ships became larger and larger. Some of the most notable examples were the *Titanic* (46,000 tons), the *Mauretania* (44,000 tons), the German

CARAVEL   GALLEON   CLIPPER

Europa (46,000 tons), the French *Normandie* (83,000 tons), the great Cunard liners, the *Queen Mary* (81,235 tons) and the *Queen Elizabeth* (85,000 tons).

The great ships of today are built of steel and aluminium. A modern ocean liner has swimming pools, lounges, theatres, dining rooms, music rooms, libraries and comfortable cabins. Some of these ships are longer than several football pitches and carry more than two thousand passengers

Not all ocean-going ships carry passengers. Many of them are freighters, or cargo ships. Special ships called tankers are used to carry oil and other liquids.

A modern ship may run on steam or diesel engines. There are also some ships that run on atomic power. Whatever the source, the power is used to turn one or more propellers.

Although the ship is steered by a wheel, the wheel is actually used to turn the *rudder*. The rudder runs down into the water from the stern of the ship.

Almost every modern ship has a *gyro-compass*, which indicates direction by the freely moving axis of a rapidly spinning wheel. Owing to the rotation of the Earth, the axis assumes and maintains a north and south direction.

Many of the great ocean-going passenger liners are fitted with stabilizers which reduce the amount of rolling and keep ships relatively steady. These stabilizers are controlled by a *gyroscope*.

There are about 40,000 commercial ships in service in the world today.

See also: BARGE; BOAT; CLIPPER SHIP; FERRY BOAT; GALLEON; GALLEY; JUNK; NUCLEAR SHIP; RAFT; SAILING SHIPS AND BOATS; SAMPAN; SCHOONER; STEAMSHIP; SUBMARINE; TANKER; WARSHIP; WINDJAMMER; YACHT.

PADDLE SHIP *SIRIUS*

A MODERN OCEAN LINER

Skis

A ski is a long, narrow, flat runner that is curved up at the front end. A pair of skis, attached to the feet, allow the wearer to glide swiftly down a snowy slope.

Traditionally, skis were made of wood, but now they are also made of fibreglass, light metals and other materials. They are three or four inches wide and should be about one foot longer than the skier's height to get maximum speed.

Ski-ing is popular as a sport in almost every country where there is plenty of snow. At first, however, it was not a sport but an important means of transport. A museum in Stockholm, Sweden, has a pair of skis that are 5,000 years old.

During the Battle of Oslo, in the year 1200, the Norwegians used skiers as scouts. The use of skis in war has continued. The Allies used ski troops during World War II, and most armies have a few soldiers who are also skilled skiers.

Ski Lift

Ski lifts are used in holiday resorts to pull skiers to the top of the slopes used for ski runs. They consist of a continuous cable from which are suspended a series of handgrips. A skier wishing to ascend the slope merely grips the handle and is then pulled along on his skis by the movement of the cable. There are also *T-bar* ski lifts against which the skier leans and is pushed up the ski slopes.

See also: CABLE CAR; CHAIR LIFT; FUNICULAR.

Sledge

A sledge (or sled, as it is sometimes called) is a vehicle that moves on runners, instead of wheels. Crude sledges, made of several tree branches lashed together, were man's first transport device. From them there developed much bigger sledges, drawn by horses and other animals.

In North America the Indians used to make *toboggan* sledges that resembled canoes on runners. The Pilgrim Fathers made sledges too but they did it very simply—they just attached runners to a box.

In about 1870, the children's sledge became popular. Later, two

An Eskimo "Nome" sledge in Canada's Northwest Territory

sledges were fastened together end to end to hold more people. This became the *bobsleigh*. The driver sat in front and steered with a rope, a wheel or a crossbar. Bobsleighs of more complicated design are used for sport.

In the Arctic Circle, where the ground is covered with snow and ice all the time, sledges are still an important means of transport. Sometimes they are the only vehicles that can move goods or people. Often the sledges are pulled by teams of dogs.

In Alaska the *Nome* sledge is commonly used. It is long and narrow, and has basket-weave sides. A team of strong dogs can haul a load of 1,000 pounds in such a sledge.

The *Nansen* sledge, made of wood tied together with rawhide, is lighter and wider. It can carry a load of 600 pounds.

Big sledges, used by scientific expeditions in Antarctica, are often pulled by tractors or *Sno-cats*.

See also: SLEIGH.

Sleigh

A sleigh is a special form of light sledge designed to carry people. Sleighs are usually pulled by horses and are used when conditions are too snowy and slippery for wheeled vehicles. Sleighs have light runners with a big curve at the front, and the passenger seat is often a foot or more above the surface.

Snowmobile

A snowmobile is an extra-large ski powered by a motor cycle engine. A small runner at the front enables the snowmobile to be steered. It may be considered a motor bicycle designed for use on snow.

Snowmobiling is one of the latest sports in the United States and Canada. At first snowmobiles had small engines giving them a speed of 20 to 30 miles an hour, but the latest models can travel at over 100 miles an hour. Fast snowmobiling is a highly skilled and dangerous sport.

Spacecraft

Spacecraft are Man's latest, most complicated and most expensive means of transport. Spacecraft are used to carry men and instruments in orbit round the Earth and to transport men and equipment to the Moon and planets.

Most spacecraft are unmanned, that is, they carry instruments only and do all their work automatically or on command from the Earth. Such spacecraft can land equipment such as television cameras and wheeled vehicles gently on the Moon, and they can carry cameras and other instruments hundreds of millions of miles to the planets Venus and Mars.

Some spacecraft are manned, that is, they carry one or more men. Up to now such spacecraft have carried men into space round the Earth, and to the Moon, but in time there is little doubt that improved models will transport men to the planets.

The spacecraft age began on 4th October, 1957, when Russia launched an artificial satellite, Sputnik 1. On 12th April, 1961, Yuri Gagarin, a Russian, was the first man to circle the earth in a spacecraft. The first

(Right) An Atlas-Agena blasts off

*(Below) Saturn V rocket with
Apollo moonship in position*

American to orbit the earth was John H. Glenn, who made three orbits in February, 1962.

A spacecraft has to be launched by a rocket. Once it has escaped from the Earth's atmosphere, the craft can coast in orbit, or continue on a set course. Control jets make it possible for the astronaut to turn the spacecraft or make it roll.

A spacecraft, like a submarine, must carry its own supply of oxygen to permit the crew to breathe. It must have machinery to remove body wastes and to control the temperature. It has to provide protection from micrometeorites, cosmic rays and the dangerous radiations coming from the Sun. If the spacecraft is designed to return to Earth, it must be heavily insulated with special materials so that it does not burn up when it re-enters the Earth's atmosphere.

In addition to all the equipment needed to protect the life and comfort

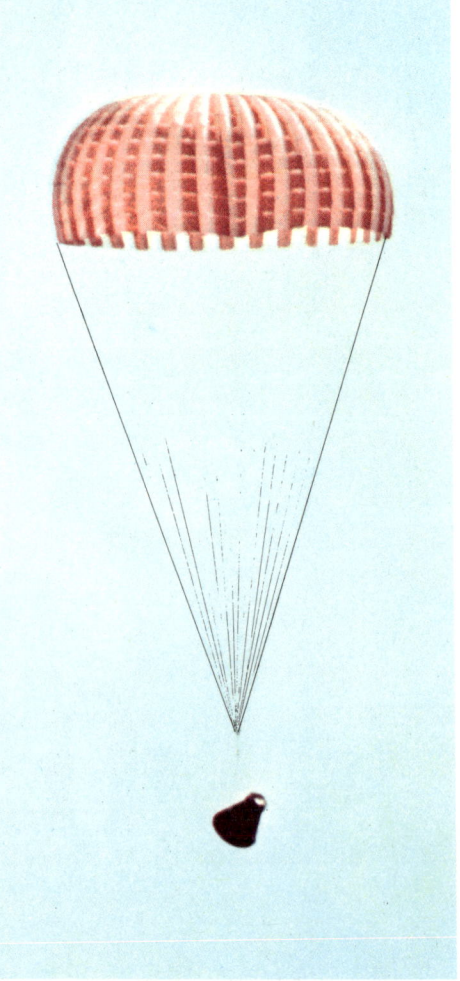

of the astronauts, the craft must have communication systems so that it can keep in touch with the Earth at all times.

Spacecraft may come down on land or in the water. The former method is used by Russian spacecraft, but American spacecraft are designed to touch down in water. In both cases parachutes are used to lower the craft the last few thousand feet.

The spacecraft of today are very complicated and expensive—or rather the rockets which launch them are—because they are used only once. The huge first stage of the Saturn rocket used to launch America's Apollo spacecraft burns only a few minutes and then falls back into the sea.

To save this waste, engineers are designing a new, re-usable booster. This will boost the spacecraft up to the desired orbital speed, and then return to Earth, landing like an aeroplane, so that it can be used again.

A Sikorsky CH-4 Choctaw helicopter hovering above a Gemini space capsule

Stagecoach

The first stagecoach, that is the first coach to carry fare-paying passengers by stages along a road, at a fixed charge for each stage, is thought to have been operating in Britain about the year 1650. It ran between London and Edinburgh, a distance of nearly 400 miles.

Initially, the roads over which the stagecoaches operated were little more than a series of holes joined by deep ruts, and a journey by stagecoach was quite an experience. Passengers crowded into the vehicle, sweated in summer and shivered in winter, and were shaken to pieces all the time. However, as better roads were constructed, travel became smoother and the stagecoach grew in popularity. Two days were needed to travel from London to Oxford, and six to reach York.

Coaches used for this purpose consisted of a heavy closed compartment, mounted on springs and drawn by either four or six horses. They usually had seats for from four to eight people, and freight and mail were carried on the roof.

See also: CARRIAGE; CHARIOT; COACH; COVERED WAGON; WAGON.

Steam Carriage

Until the invention of the steam carriage, all vehicles had been pulled by horses or other animals. But the steam carriages had their own engines; they moved themselves.

The first steam-driven vehicle was built in 1769 by Joseph Cugnot, a French artillery officer, to pull an army cannon. It was a strange looking thing, with two rear wheels and one at the front; overhanging the front wheel was the bulky boiler. Its top speed was about 2 miles an hour, and the steam only lasted fifteen minutes. At the end of that time the vehicle had to stop until it built up enough steam to go again. It was not very successful.

The first British steam carriage was built in 1800 by Richard Trevithick, an engineer from Cornwall. This looked like an early railway engine, except that it ran along the road instead of on rails. In 1803 Trevithick built an improved carriage, and like the stagecoach it had a body mounted between two enormous wooden driving wheels twelve feet in diameter.

During the next fifty years several steam carriages were built and some of these, just like the buses of today, carried passengers regularly.

In 1831, a six-wheeled steam carriage built by Sir Goldsworthy Gurney ran a service between Cheltenham and Gloucester, carrying 3,000 passengers in four months. The most successful service of all was one

Steam carriage, 1833—this one held 56 people

operated by Walter Hancock, who built ten vehicles and ran them between Paddington and the City of London for eight years.

However, most of these steam carriages were not very efficient. They were dirty, and often ran out of steam and fuel. Sometimes the boiler exploded.

Also, they were disliked by the operators of horse-drawn vehicles who naturally feared that the steam engine might ruin their livelihood, and they took violent action against it; for example, the service operated by the Gurney steam carriage was stopped by piling loose stones all along the road. Further restrictive measures included high road tolls for steam vehicles. And the final blow came in 1865, when the government passed the regulation known as "The Red Flag Act". This law required that every road vehicle must have a "crew" of three, including one person to walk in front carrying a red flag. The maximum speed permitted was 4 miles an hour.

Up to this time British steam carriages were among the best in the world, but when the Red Flag Act became law, progress in Britain virtually stopped overnight. Not only did the law kill the steam carriage, it severely delayed the development of the petrol-driven motor car in this country.

See also: MOTOR CAR.

Steam Locomotive

A steam locomotive uses the energy of steam as the source of its power. The steam is made by heating water, usually by burning coal or oil. Steam takes up much more space than water. As it expands, or spreads out, its energy is used to push pistons which are enclosed in cylinders. Valves direct the steam to push the pistons first in one direction, then the

A wood-burning locomotive built in the United States in 1864

The BULKELEY—*locomotives similar to this provided the power for the trains of the Great Western Railway for over three decades, until April, 1892.*

other, and finally allow the steam to escape. A system of piston rods and connecting rods turn the locomotive's wheels.

The story of the steam engine is an old one. The first one that we know of was made by Hero of Alexandria about 120 B.C. His steam engine was basically a hollow globe with two pipes. When steam spouted from the pipes, it caused the globe to whirl around. The engine was a curiosity and it was not used for any practical purpose.

In 1698, Thomas Savery invented a steam engine to pump water from mines. In 1705, Thomas Newcomen designed a more elaborate steam engine with a piston and cylinder, using the pressure of the atmosphere, rather than steam pressure as in Savery's engine, as the driving force. Newcomen improved Savery's primitive steam engine and in 1725 built a practical working engine for use in collieries. These early engines were inefficient and wasted large amounts of fuel.

The steam engine became commercially important in 1769 with the inventions of James Watt, a Scotsman. Watt's engine had a cylinder which remained hot all the time. This engine used only about one-fourth as much fuel as Newcomen's engine. Watt also developed the *double-action* engine. The steam was used first on one side of the piston to push it down, then on the other to push it back. Before long, the steam engine was being used for purposes other than pumping.

In 1804, Richard Trevithick built his steam locomotive. It weighed five tons and hauled a load of nearly twenty tons at 5 miles an hour. The locomotive itself was successful but had to be abandoned because the cast-iron rails of its track were not strong enough to support it. A few years later, Trevithick built another locomotive which ran on a circular track. It pulled one carriage and the train was called *Catch Me Who Can*. People paid a fare to ride on the gadget while it raced round at the startling speed of 12 miles an hour.

There were other locomotives and other improvements, but the next great milestone came with the *Blucher*, a steam locomotive built by George Stephenson, another Englishman, in 1814. The *Blucher* drew an eight-carriage train at a speed of 4 miles an hour. Stephenson continued to make improvements and in 1829 he built the *Rocket*. This locomotive

The CITY OF TRURO—*the first locomotive to exceed 100 m.p.h.*

was such a success that Stephenson is generally thought of as the father of the modern steam locomotive.

Within a short period, railways began to grow in Europe and in America. Many improvements were made to the steam locomotive, but its basic principles remained the same.

Today the steam engine has been replaced in most countries by the cleaner and more efficient electric and diesel-electric locomotives. But it was the steam locomotive which made railways possible, and which led to the development of the vast railway systems in operation today all over the world.

See also: DIESEL-ELECTRIC LOCOMOTIVE; DIESEL-HYDRAULIC LOCO-MOTIVE; ELECTRIC LOCOMOTIVE; RAILWAY.

Steamship

In 1783, a small French boat powered by steam made a fifteen-minute trip on the River Saône. Five years later a Scottish engineer called William Symington, aided by another Scot called Patrick Miller, made a steam-boat which reached a speed of 5 miles an hour. This is considered to be the world's first practical steamship.

Later Symington built an improved steamship, named the *Charlotte Dundas*. Robert Fulton, an American, went for a trip in her. He realized that such ships could be used to carry merchandise or passengers cheaply upstream against strong currents, and returned to America to build steamships. His first, the *Clermont*, was launched in 1807 and steamed upriver from New York to Albany and back again.

Like nearly all early steamships, the Fulton vessels were driven by paddles. Usually these were located in the middle of the ship, one either side, so that by reversing one wheel they could help to turn the ship. Those used on the Mississippi, however, usually had a large single paddle at the rear and are sometimes called *stern-wheelers*. Stern-wheelers were ideal for use in shallow inland waterways.

The great Cunarder QUEEN ELIZABETH *made her last voyage across the Atlantic in 1968*

Elsewhere the steamship was also gaining ground. In 1819, the *Savannah*, an American ship, crossed the Atlantic Ocean in one month, using steam part of the time and sails the rest. This voyage was completely overshadowed by that of the British ship, the S.S. *Sirius*, which arrived in New York on 26th April, 1838, to start passenger services across the Atlantic. The little *Sirius*, loaded down with 94 passengers, had been built for use in the Irish Channel. But she crossed the Atlantic entirely under steam, although she burned up all her coal—most of the cabin doors and furniture, and even one mast!

Four hours later the *Great Western*, built by the famous British engineer and designer, Isambard Brunel, steamed into New York. She had only eight passengers but plenty of coal left and was the first real transatlantic steamship. She was followed by others, including Brunel's handsome *Great Britain* of 1843, which had a revolutionary iron hull and a screw propeller and could carry 260 passengers and 1,200 tons of freight.

Not only were steamships proving faster and more reliable than sailing ships, they were more comfortable. As far back as 1809 the *Clermont* had 54 armchairs for passengers to relax in during the night run to Albany. The splendour of the rich furnishings and decoration of the cabins on the early Mississippi stern-wheelers has seldom been surpassed. The ocean-going steamship also had plenty of space, at least for the first-class passengers.

The tradition is continued today. The biggest steamships, or liners as we now call them, are floating cities, with swimming pools, lounges, theatres, great dining-rooms, music rooms, libraries and comfortable cabins.

One of the most famous—but least successful—steamships was the *Great Eastern*, designed by Brunel. Launched in 1858 she ruined the line that built her, and as a passenger-carrying ship was a failure. She was an iron ship, displacing 22,600 tons, with a double hull and equipped with both paddle-wheels and a propeller. She could carry 4,000 passengers, but seldom did, as she rolled violently on the Atlantic run and had to be taken out of service two years later.

As a steamship, however, the *Great Eastern* was half a century ahead of her time. Her tonnage was not equalled until 1904.

Today, more and more merchant ships and liners are turning away from steam to diesel power—threatening to end the reign of the steamship in a little over one hundred years after its first triumphs.

See also: SHIP; WARSHIP.

Submarine

A submarine is a vessel that can travel below the surface of water. It can also move on the surface, like an ordinary ship.

Early designs for submarines extend back to the early 1600s, and crude submarines were tried out during the American War of Independence and the Civil War, but with little success.

Submarines are complicated boats to design and make, particularly the underwater navigation equipment, and it was not until the end of the nineteenth century that engineering had advanced sufficiently to enable the problems to be solved.

The first practical submarine was credited to Robert Fulton who built one in 1765. He demonstrated it to both France and England during the Napoleonic Wars but neither country was interested. It was well into the nineteenth century before the American, John Holland, perfected a large fighting submarine.

The *Holland* is generally considered to be the first modern-style submarine. The *Holland* was actually lighter than water, and was forced under water by its steering vanes. It had a petrol engine for cruising on the surface and an electric motor for submerged running. Britain was the last of the major powers to order a Holland boat, in 1901.

It was the Germans, in 1914, who first used submarines as a powerful weapon of war. At one period German *U-boats* (short for *Unterseeboot*) were sinking 500,000 tons of Allied shipping a month.

When it is sailing on the surface of the water, a submarine is much like any other ship. Its shape is something like that of a cigar or a fish. In order to submerge, or sink below the surface, tanks along its sides fill with water. These are called ballast tanks. When it has taken in enough water, the submarine is heavy enough to sink. The hull of a submarine has to be unusually strong to withstand the pressure of water on it. At a depth of 200 feet, this pressure is 88·9 pounds per square inch. By filling and emptying its tanks, a submarine can go all the way down to the bottom of the sea, part way down, or remain just below the surface.

Sectional diagrams of a manpowered submarine, the HUNLEY, *which saw service in the American Civil War*

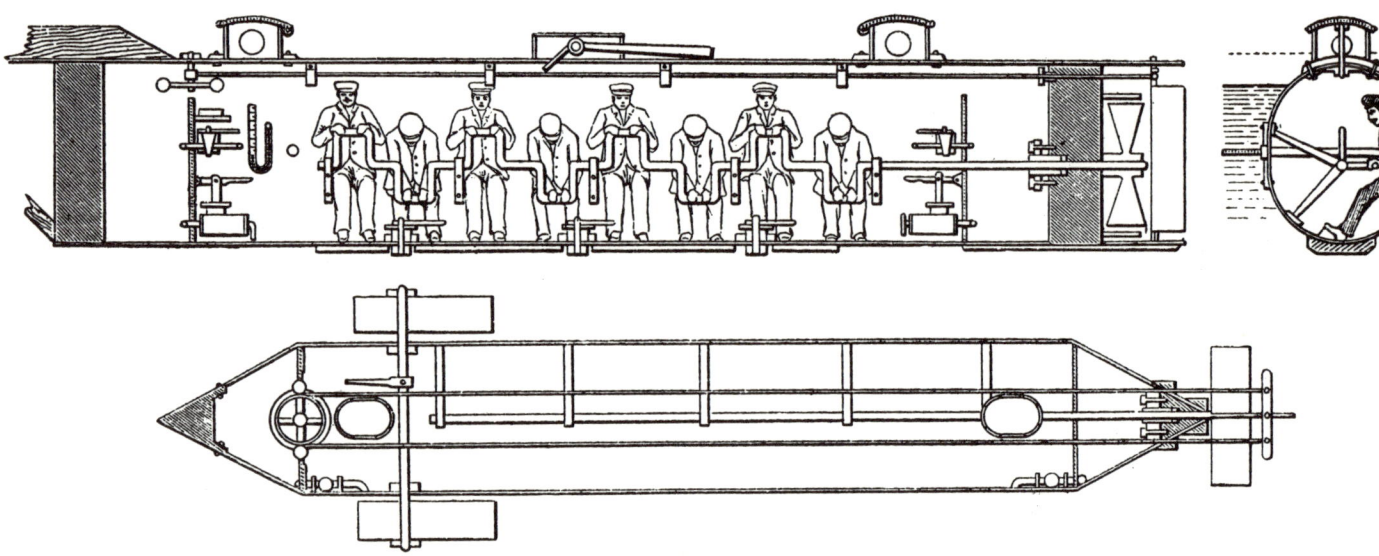

When it is time to surface, the water is blown out of the ballast tanks by air pressure.

Although it may use any kind of power on the surface, a submarine in a dive may use only a form of power that does not need air. This means that no engine that burns fuel can be used.

Until recently, the usual power for submarines was electricity from huge storage batteries. The length of time a submarine could stay down was limited by the amount of electricity it could store.

This problem was solved with the development of nuclear submarines. These use atomic power. The fuel produces so much energy and takes up so little space that nuclear submarines can remain submerged for months at a time.

The first nuclear-powered submarine was the American *Nautilus*, which was completed in 1955. It sailed under the thick sheet of ice covering the North Pole in 1958. In 1960, the *Triton* circumnavigated the world, remaining under water all the time. It travelled 41,500 miles in 84 days.

Today, both the United States and the U.S.S.R. have large fleets of nuclear-powered submarines, many of which carry rockets armed with atomic warheads.

Submarines are not used solely for war. Special submarines are used by scientists to explore the bottom of the sea. They also assist in the underwater salvage of shipwrecks and in offshore oil and gas drilling operations. Some experts also feel that merchant submarines will be built in the future. Cruising under the surface they would be unaffected by storms and rough seas.

See also: SHIP; WARSHIP.

Tanker

A Leyland "Lynx" 16-ton milk tanker

Tanker is the term given to both road vehicles and ships built specially to transport petrol and other fuel oils.

A road tanker is basically a large cylindrical drum mounted on wheels, with the driving cab at the front. Road tankers distribute nearly all the petrol required for motor cars and lorries, and the fuel required for central heating in houses, shops and factories.

The ship tankers are used to transport fuel oil to the countries that need it from the countries, mostly in the Middle East, where it is pumped out of the ground. These tankers, with the modern ore and bulk carriers, are by far the largest ships ever built. They are much bigger than famous passenger liners such as France's *France* and Britain's *Queen Elizabeth II*. These liners are of 65,000 tons gross, but tankers are of 100,000, 200,000 and even 300,000 tons gross, and are more than a third of a mile long. A monster of 500,000 tons gross is under construction, and there is talk of one being designed to carry 1,000,000 tons of oil on one trip.

Road tankers and ship tankers play a most important part in the story of transport.

Taxi

A taxi, short for taxi cab, is a small road vehicle which can be hired by people to carry them to a particular destination. A taxi cab can be an ordinary motor car, fitted with a sign indicating its purpose and a taxi-meter which measures time and distance to calculate the fare. But special taxi cabs are made; these usually have a space beside the driver for extra luggage. They can also turn in a very small circle so that they can manoeuvre easily in traffic and narrow streets.

Taxis usually work in towns and cities, and carry people to and from hotels, theatres, restaurants and airport terminals. They are not usually used for long journeys.

Tracked Vehicles

Most vehicles designed for use on land have wheels to enable them to move about easily and smoothly. Wheels are ideal when the ground is hard and dry, but they are not suitable on areas which are muddy, very rough, or soft and sandy.

To enable vehicles to cross this type of ground a special device called a track is used. A track is a form of belt which lays a continuous path down for the vehicle to move along on. After the vehicle has passed over the length of track on the ground, it is picked up and carried forward, when it is laid down again, so that the process can be repeated.

FV 432 armoured personnel carrier

A Scotsman, Andrew Dunlop, built a "footed wheel" in 1861. However, in 1882, a design by Fender of Buenos Aires—a chain track driven by a hexagonal sprocket—was perhaps the true forerunner of present day track layouts.

By the turn of the century tracked farm vehicles, with their ability to cross rough ground, were in widespread use in the United States.

The military potential of tracked vehicles was not overlooked. In 1908 the British War Office offered a prize of £1,000 for a cross-country vehicle that could haul a load forty miles without the need to refuel. Tracked vehicles, code-named "tanks", to prevent the enemy guessing their purpose, were used for the first time by the British during the Great War of 1914–18. Their appearance surprised both friend and foe, but the gaps they made in the enemy lines of trenches were not exploited fully, so that their success was not as great as it could have been.

The name tank has continued to be used for this class of tracked fighting vehicle armed with cannon and machine guns.

Because of their great weight, and because the nature of their duties makes it necessary for them to be able to cross rough and soft ground, all tanks have tracks.

Tracks are expensive, compared with wheels, and are thus generally used only on military vehicles and specialized vehicles that need to operate over rough ground. The most common tracked vehicle we can see is the bulldozer, used to help build roads and on building sites. Tracked cranes are also often seen in such places.

See also: CRAWLER.

Train Ferry *See Boat Train*

Tram

A tram is basically an electrically-operated bus which moves along tracks, like a train. Power is obtained from an underground rail or overhead cable.

The earliest trams, called streetcars in the United States, were drawn by horses and were known as *horsecars*. The first electric tram was put into use in Germany in 1881, and before long electric trams began to replace horsecars everywhere.

A modern tramcar, New Orleans, Louisiana, U.S.A.

At one time, trams were the most important means of transport in cities, and between cities and towns that were close together. But the fact that they move on rails restricts their versatility; the rails are a hazard for pedestrians, motor cars and bicycles. Because of this many cities, such as London and Glasgow, have replaced their trams with ordinary buses.

See also: BUS; TROLLEY BUS.

Trap

A trap is a small, light, two-wheeled vehicle, drawn either by a horse or

pony. At one time traps were used much like a motor car is today, that is, for visiting friends or going shopping.

One can still see the occasional trap along country roads in some parts of Britain.

See also: CARRIAGE; COACH; STAGECOACH; WAGON.

Travois

A travois is a primitive device for transporting loads. It consists of a platform or net slung between two poles, the upper ends of which are hitched to an animal while the lower ends drag along the ground. Travois were extensively used by American Indians.

See also: SLEDGE.

Trimaran

A trimaran is a vessel consisting of three hulls joined together by a rigid frame.

Trimaran sailing vessels, consisting of a large central hull and two smaller outriggers, are popular because of their great stability, high speed, and space for crew and provisions.

See also: CATAMARAN; YACHT.

Troika

Of Russian origin, a troika is a vehicle drawn by a team of three horses harnessed abreast of each other.

Trolley Bus

A trolley bus is an electrically-operated bus which obtains its power from overhead power lines. Trolley buses have a rapid acceleration which makes them ideal for use in cities where stops are frequent. However, the disadvantage of being able to run only where there are power lines restrict their versatility, and trolley buses are not often used today.

See also: BUS; TRAM.

A troika

Umiak

A umiak is an open boat used by Eskimo women. With an average length of thirty feet and a beam of eight feet, it is made of a wooden frame covered with skins. The women use broad paddles to propel the umiak through the water.

See also: CANOE; KAYAK.

Underground

An underground, known as a subway in some countries, is a railway that runs under the ground. In crowded cities it is a great advantage to have an underground system which can transport tens of thousands of people an hour without adding to the traffic on the streets above.

The first underground in the world was opened in London in 1863. It used steam locomotives, and the air in the tunnels and stations was foul beyond belief. Engineers, however, soon turned to electricity, and today all underground trains are powered by electricity supplied from a third rail near the track. The power reaches the motor of the train through a metal plate called a *shoe* which slides along the third rail. Underground railways have stations at intervals along the route. If the station is not too far below the surface, passengers can reach it by going down a flight of stairs. When it is very deep, the station may be reached by escalators and lifts.

Some underground railways are made by cutting a deep trench, building the tunnel at the bottom and then filling in the trench when it is finished. These stretches of underground usually have rectangular tunnels.

Most undergrounds, however, are made by boring through the earth from under the surface. These undergrounds have round, or semi-circular tunnels. This method was used on the new Victoria Line, the latest addition to London's vast and complex system of underground railways.

Moscow has an underground railway which is famous for its elaborately decorated stations. These contain fine works of sculpture and some have marble floors and crystal chandeliers.

See also: ELECTRIC LOCOMOTIVE; RAILWAY.

A station on the famous Moscow underground

Tilt wing VTOL airliner—the McDonald XC 142 A

VTOL

VTOL stands for Vertical Take Off and Landing, and is one of the latest methods of transport. The term covers aircraft which, unlike present day airliners, do not need miles of concrete runway when landing or taking off. A VTOL airliner can land or take off vertically from a small patch of concrete.

Helicopters have always been able to do this, and are thus VTOLs, but helicopters are complicated and relatively slow. The term VTOL is generally applied to a brand new type of airliner which can rise straight up like a helicopter, and then fly forward in fast level flight like an ordinary airliner. The term *convertiplane* is sometimes used instead of VTOL.

Engineers have several ways of achieving VTOL. One method is to arrange for the whole wing to tilt up. For take off, the wing is tilted so that the engines are pointing straight up, and the aircraft takes off like a helicopter. At the desired height the wing is tilted forward and the aircraft then flies like a conventional airliner. At the destination, the wing is tilted up again and the aircraft lands like a helicopter.

127

Another method is to fit separate engines to lift the aircraft up. These "lift" engines, as they are called, can be fitted in big pods on the wings, or in a row down each side of the fuselage. For take-off only the lift engines are used. At the desired height the main engines are started, to push the aircraft along. When sufficient speed is reached for the wings to support the aircraft, the lift engines are switched off. At the destination the process is reversed.

In a period when airports are becoming even more crowded and farther and farther from cities, VTOL airliners have many benefits. They could increase the capacity of normal airports, reduce noise and, in time, enable passengers to land in the middle of cities. This would help to reduce the time spent in travelling from most airports to the centres of the cities they serve.

See also: AIRLINER; AUTOGYRO; HELICOPTER.

Wagon

In the Middle Ages, although there were many crude roads, transport had not developed much beyond the use of two-wheeled carts pulled by horses or oxen.

One of the reasons for this slow development was the inefficient methods used to harness horses to their vehicles. Based on Roman ideas, the pulling was usually done by a harness strap which passed round the breast of the horse. This tightened on its throat as soon as it moved for-

A Conestoga wagon

128

ward, thus strangling the animal. It seems incredible that the Romans, who were skilled engineers, never invented an efficient harness.

The invention, the rigid horse-collar, pressed against the shoulders of the animal, enabling it to pull without pressure on its windpipe. The new invention spread slowly, but in the end it was of great importance. It helped to revolutionize transport and to usher in the era of stagecoaches which helped to lay the foundations of our modern world.

Perhaps the most common horse-drawn vehicle, however, was the wagon. This is the term generally applied to any four-wheeled horse-drawn vehicle, used primarily for carrying freight, merchandise or heavy goods. There is a great variety of wagons, the best known being those rugged wooden vehicles used on farms.

Wagons played an important part in the settlement of the American West. The pioneers needed a vehicle which would not only carry their precious possessions, but would provide protection against attack and be, in effect, a mobile home.

One of the most popular wagons was the *Conestoga*, named after the town in Pennsylvania where it was first built. The wagon body was raised high above the ground, the ends being turned upwards and higher than in the centre. This shape kept the five-ton load from falling out. The cargo and occupants were protected by a canvas covering stretched over curved wooden ribs, to form an arched enclosure. Because of this canvas, the wagons are often referred to as covered wagons. Conestoga wagons were drawn by four to eight horses or oxen.

For greater safety, pioneers used to travel in groups of a hundred people or more, the line of wagons involved being known as a wagon train.

See also: CARRIAGE; CHARIOT; COACH; COVERED WAGON; STAGECOACH.

Warship

A warship is a ship that is designed for fighting. In the world of transport their task may be considered as that of carrying men and guns to within range of enemy targets. A warship may be a tiny boat with one man in it, or a huge aircraft carrier carrying squadrons of fighter and bomber aeroplanes. Over the centuries, there have been warships of many kinds.

One of the earliest warships appears in a stone carving by an Assyrian about 3,000 years ago. The prow of the ship carried a long, sharp pole that was used to ram other ships. The sides of the ship were protected by animal hides.

The ancient Greeks and Romans used galleys as warships. The Vikings of A.D. 1000 used long ships called *drakkars*, or dragons. Galleys and drakkars were powered by oars. Sea battles were fought by ramming and sinking the enemy, or by steering alongside and sending soldiers aboard.

From the fifteenth century, warships began to carry guns. The Spaniards of the fifteenth and sixteenth centuries had heavy clumsy warships called galleons, sometimes with several rows of guns on each side. When the Spanish navy set out to defeat the English in 1588, the heavy galleons proved to be no match for the lighter, easy-to-handle English ships. The Spanish navy was defeated, and warship design began to change quickly. Ships became more manoeuvrable, and large enough to carry many guns.

The frigate was the main warship of the seventeenth and eighteenth centuries. One of the most famous frigates was the American *Constitution* which was launched in 1797. This was bigger than existing frigates and distinguished itself in several individual combats. The best known British warship of this period is, of course, the *Victory*, which was Nelson's flagship at the Battle of Trafalgar. The *Victory*, restored to her original condition, can be seen in Portsmouth Dockyard.

During the American Civil War, two iron-clad ships, the *Monitor* and the *Merrimac*, were built. They fought a battle in 1862. Neither ship clearly won the fight, but it did prove that the time of the wooden ship was over. From this time on, iron or steel ships with movable gun turrets were made.

In 1906 H.M.S. *Dreadnought* was completed for the British Navy. It weighed 18,000 tons and carried ten 12-inch guns, and made all other warships obsolete. For many years battleships of all navies were patterned on the *Dreadnought*.

Smaller ships, called destroyers, also made their appearance. They were heavily armed but smaller, lighter and faster than battleships. They were capable of launching torpedoes and depth charges.

During World War II landing craft were used extensively for the first time. These can come very close to shore to land men and supplies.

The aircraft carrier also became very important. This is a huge ship with a very large deck that can act as a landing field for aeroplanes. In its day the aircraft carrier was considered the capital ship, that is the most important, of a navy, taking the position formerly held by the battleship.

Today, many people consider that the position of capital ship has passed to the nuclear-powered submarine, with its deadly load of rockets armed with atomic warheads.

See also: GALLEON; GALLEY; SAILING SHIPS AND BOATS; SHIP; STEAMSHIP; SUBMARINE.

HEAVY CRUISER

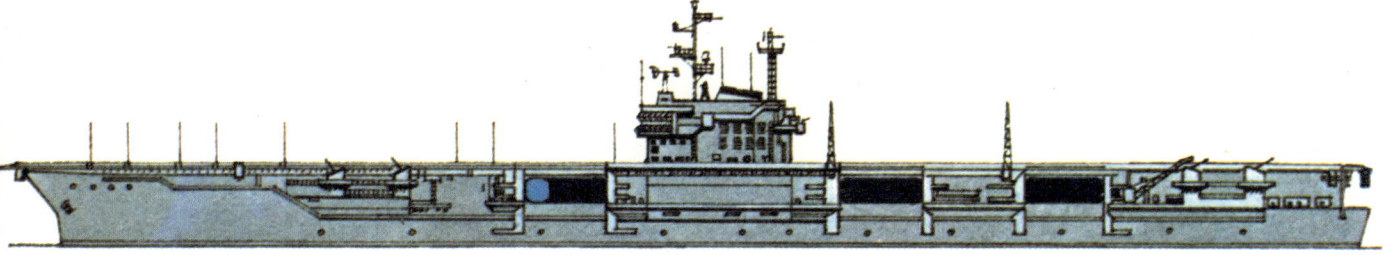

AIRCRAFT CARRIER

DESTROYER

SUBMARINE

GERMAN POCKET BATTLESHIP

BATTLESHIP

MINESWEEPER

MOTOR TORPEDO BOAT

Windjammer

Windjammers were large three, four or five-masted, iron-hulled sailing cargo vessels, built strictly for economy and used mainly on routes rounding Cape Horn. They represented a last fling by sailing craft against the steamship, and survived into this century. Now, like the beautiful clipper ships which preceded them, they are relics of the past.

See also: CLIPPER SHIP; SAILING SHIPS AND BOATS; SCHOONER.

Yacht

A yacht is a vessel that is used only for pleasure. Yachts have a graceful shape and are usually powered by sails, although a motor may be fitted.

Sailing yachts were introduced to Britain by King Charles II, who built twenty-six of them and used them not only for royal business but also for pleasure and racing. The name seems to have come from the Dutch *jacht* —a small, fast, lightly-armed sailing craft which was often used for state business such as transporting important people.

See also: SAILING SHIPS AND BOATS.

Zeppelin

Zeppelin is the general name given to a series of large rigid airships, built by a German army officer, Count Ferdinand von Zeppelin.

The first of these graceful aerial giants, the *L.Z.1*, was launched in 1900. It was 420 feet long with two engines which developed a total of 32 horse-power, and it could cruise at about 20 miles an hour. From it developed a whole series of remarkable Zeppelins.

In 1910 Zeppelins began regular passenger-carrying flights between various German cities. Thus, five Zeppelins began a service which, during the next four years, was to carry over 35,000 passengers some 170,000 miles, without a single fatality or injury.

Nearly seventy Zeppelins were built during World War I, some of which were used on raids against Britain. The fighting qualities of these vulnerable highly-inflammable ships were poor. On the other hand, they were extremely valuable for maritime patrol and reconnaissance duties.

In 1928 the most famous Zeppelin of all was built—the *Graf Zeppelin*, or *L.Z.127*—nearly 800 feet long and of finely streamlined form with a maximum diameter of 100 feet. In 1929 this great airship flew round the world, covering 21,500 miles in 21 days, including 7,000 miles non-stop from Friedrichshaven to Tokyo; an outstanding achievement. The *Graf Zeppelin* then began a regular transatlantic service. Altogether it made over 600 journeys, including 100 ocean crossings, flew over 1,200,000 miles and carried nearly 14,000 passengers before being honourably retired in 1937.

Her place was taken by the *Hindenberg*, which accommodated 72 passengers in surroundings as comfortable and as elegant as those of a luxury ocean-going liner. Over 800 feet long it made 54 trips including 36 Atlantic crossings. On 5th May, 1936, when coming in to land at Lakehurst, New Jersey, after a flight from Germany, the great ship suddenly burst into flames. Thirty-six people lost their lives. The public lost confidence in these craft and the era of the Zeppelin came to an end.

See also: AIRSHIP; BALLOON; BLIMP; DIRIGIBLE.

The wreckage of a Zeppelin, shot down during a bombing raid in World War I

Index

(Page numbers in italics are illustrations)

James Watt

George Stephenson

Joseph Montgolfier

Robert Fulton

Alan B. Shepard, Jr.

Henri Giffard

Elisha Graves Otis